THE BRIDLED TONGUE

THE BRIDLED TONGUE

Bible Words About Words

Selected by

FLORENCE M. TAYLOR

Keats Publishing, Inc.   New Canaan, Connecticut

Grateful acknowledgement is made to the following for their generous permission to reprint from these copyrighted works:

Harper & Row, Publishers, Inc., for the excerpt from
FOUNDATIONS FOR RECONSTRUCTION by Elton Trueblood,
© 1948 by Elton Trueblood.

Wm. B. Eerdmans Publishing Co., for the excerpt from
SPIRITUAL DEPRESSION: ITS CAUSES AND CURE by D. Martyn
Lloyd-Jones, © 1965 by Wm. B. Eerdmans Publishing Co.

ISBN: 0-87983-115-4
LIBRARY OF CONGRESS CATALOG CARD NUMBER 75-19545

PRINTED IN THE UNITED STATES OF AMERICA

KEATS PUBLISHING, INC.
36 GROVE STREET, NEW CANAAN, CONNECTICUT 06840

THIS BOOK IS
DEDICATED TO THE MEMORY OF
"BILL"
(THE LATE DR. WILLIAM A. LEATH)
IN LOVING AND GRATEFUL
APPRECIATION OF WHAT HIS MINISTRY
AND HIS FAITHFUL
INTERPRETATION OF GOD'S WORD
HAVE MEANT TO ME
FOR ALMOST FIFTY YEARS

CONTENTS

INTRODUCTION

I remember, back when I was about eleven years old, attending a neighborhood Bible club. At the close of each session we were given a little strip of paper on which was written a Bible verse that we were supposed to memorize during the coming week.

Trudging home, I would tuck the slip of paper in my pants pocket and try to recall the verse. It was tempting to pull it out and check on myself, but I tried to resist the temptation as long as I could. I didn't want to resort to the little slip until I absolutely had to.

It was doubly hard to implant God's Word in your heart when you were also trying to avoid stepping on cracks in the sidewalk.

There was one verse that was particularly difficult for me to memorize. To this day, I have a hard time quoting it. But it's a good verse, nevertheless.

Here it is: "A good word fitly spoken is like apples of gold in pictures of silver" (Proverbs 25:11).

Maybe eleven-year-old boys are more interested in balls of pigskin and cowhide than they are in apples of gold. Or maybe I didn't appreciate the aesthetic qualities of a picture in silver. But for some reason it seemed impossible for me to memorize that verse.

Gradually, however, in the intervening years, I have come to appreciate "fitly spoken words." And I have come to regard them as more precious than da Vinci's *Mona Lisa* and Michelangelo's *David.*

While it may be that talk is cheap, it is certain that fitly spoken words are not. Obviously Jesus Christ was of the same opinion, for He said, "Every idle word that men shall speak, they shall give account thereof in the day of judgment" (Matthew 12:36).

"Fitly spoken words" are what Florence Taylor's book is all about. And she has gone to the proper place to find her instruction—the Word of God itself.

There was another verse that I tried to memorize at the neighborhood Bible club. For some reason I was more successful in getting this one into my thick skull. It was: "He that heareth my word, and believeth on him that sent me, hath everlasting life, and shall not come into condemnation; but is passed from death unto life" (John 5:24).

As I mulled over this verse in my early years, I realized the vital importance of God's Word, not only of hearing it but also of placing my trust in the One who gave it. Believing the Word is hardly optional; it is crucial to man's future. And thus it is of "transcending importance," as Florence Taylor puts it, to study it.

I think you will be impressed, maybe even amazed, at how much the Bible has to say about words. But you shouldn't be. After all, the Bible declares itself to be the Word of God; Jesus Christ came as the Incarnate Word; the prophets called upon their listeners to "hear the Word of the Lord," and in the New Testament those who gladly received the Word were baptized and became members of the Christian Church.

From Genesis 1:3, where God uttered the words, "Let there be light," to the last invitation in Revelation 22:17, when those who hear God's Word invite others to come, the Bible is God's revelation in words.

But out of my hazy recollections of that neighborhood Bible class, I recall a third verse about words. It was: "Be ye doers of the word, and not hearers only, deceiving your own selves" (James 1:22).

INTRODUCTION

The verse in the Epistle of James appears only a few verses before the one that speaks of bridling your tongue. Since memorizing James 1:22, I have become aware that many who have heard the Word do not do the Word. And yet it is vital that the Word be applied.

That is what James was so concerned about. And it's what Florence Taylor is concerned with too.

According to James, God is not impressed with the quantity of words that spout forth from your lips, no matter how coated with religious clichés they may be. What God seeks are men and women who know how to bridle their tongues.

Some people's tongues are like wild stallions that have never known a bridle. But James tells us that unless we know how to bridle the tongue, we will never know how to bridle the rest of the body.

This book is worth more than a quick reading. Florence Taylor has arranged the scriptures in such a way that you will want to refer to this book frequently as you seek to be "a doer of the Word." It's obviously a book for meditation as well as for reading.

William J. Petersen

I said, I will take heed to my ways,
that I sin not with my tongue:
I will keep my mouth with a bridle.

PSALMS 39:1

If any man among you seem
to be religious, and bridleth not his
tongue, but deceiveth his
own heart, this man's religion is vain.

JAMES 1:26

Foreword
MIRACLE OF WORDS

I can recall the exact moment when I first became vividly aware of the miracle of words—the sheer wonder and mystery of being able to translate innermost thoughts and feelings into sounds through which they could be accurately conveyed to other persons, and the additional and related miracle of being able to transcribe certain black marks on paper which could carry these same thoughts and feelings far beyond the sound of the human voice.

I was in my early forties at the time. I was happily married, the mother of three children ranging in age from six to sixteen. The past seven years had been an important period in my life in terms of my spiritual growth. This was largely due to a young minister who had come to our church as Minister of Education. When Bill* first came, I was dutifully and quite casually involved in the Church School. When he left, seven years later, I had caught fire from his enthusiasm; my own Christian faith had been immeasurably enriched; my interest in Christian education had become a major drive in my life and had resulted in the beginning of my writing in this field.

At the end of the seven years, Bill accepted a call to a church in the Midwest; but by that time our friendship was on a solid basis not dependent on propinquity. We wrote infrequently but often enough to keep in touch.

On the particular day when I realized the miracle of words, I

---

* The late Dr. William A. Leath, to whom this book is dedicated. Minister of Education at Union Congregational Church, Upper Montclair, New Jersey, about 1928–1935.

had recently received one of Bill's letters which had moved me deeply. He had come across an article of mine in one of the religious education magazines, and he wrote to tell me how much he felt my writing had improved. In the course of his letter he said, "Whenever I see the name Florence M. Taylor in print, I feel that a small part of myself is there."

So on this particular morning, I sat at my typewriter and started a letter to him: "Dear Bill," and it was then that I was suddenly overwhelmed by the sheer wonder of what I was doing. His letter to me was in my hand; my letter to him would soon reach him. Separated by some 600 miles, the miracle of written words permitted us still to share our deepest thoughts and feelings.

I took out of the typewriter the letter I had started, and inserted a new sheet of paper on which I wrote the following prayer (which I later included in my letter):

FOR WORDS

O God of wondrous powers,
Of miracles sublime,
Life holds no greater miracle
than this:
That longings, fears, affections,
doubts and faith
Can find their way
Beyond the narrow confines
of a single heart
Out to the reaching hearts
of others;
That each one separate and alone,
Can still from solitariness

reach out
And know the breathless miracle
of understanding.

Our hearts do give thee
grateful thanks,
O God, for words!
For words, fraught with
the centuries of struggle
Of countless million men
To make articulate
The hidden dreams and longings
of their hearts;
For words, so strangely,
marvellously potent,
That, used with skill,
They can build up,
and strengthen and protect
That rare choice gift
of human brotherhood.

O God, whose Spirit, wordless,
Still communicates thy thoughts
To those in harmony with thee,
Grant that we may most carefully
employ
This mystic, strange device
which thou hast given.
Guard thou the words we speak,
The words we write,
And make of them a holy sacrament
Used only for the furtherance

Of love, and faith, and hope,
And human brotherhood,
And fellowship with thee.   Amen.

Now, some forty years later, my wonder at words has, if anything, increased, and in a very real sense this book is the
outgrowth of that moment of spiritual illumination so many
years ago.

My prayer is that every reader of these pages may share to
some degree in this insight; that he may come to a new appreciation of God's gift of words, and to a new sense of responsibility
in his use of this gift, which of all created creatures has been
given to man alone.

Florence M. Taylor

THE BRIDLED TONGUE

THE PLAN OF THE BOOK

This book is developed in three main parts and a conclusion:

PART I: OUR WORDS TO ONE ANOTHER
PART II: MY WORDS TO MYSELF
PART III: GOD'S WORDS TO US IN THE BIBLE
PART IV: CONCLUSION: GOD'S WORDS THROUGH US

I had thought, originally, of a fourth main part: OUR WORDS TO GOD. As the book developed it became obvious to me that our words to God fell naturally into the various sections, usually under the subheading "Responses."

It needs to be said, perhaps, that no words to God quoted from the Bible or from any other source, can ever be as significant as the living, spontaneous words of our hearts, with which we reach out to God in times of deep feeling—words of praise and thanksgiving, of repentance, of genuine commitment, of trust and acceptance.

The individual, nevertheless, who has nourished his faith on words of genuine prayer that have poured forth to God from his saints in all ages, has learned a language of worship which can immeasurably enrich his own times of prayer.

Do you remember the story of the two men standing on the brink of the Grand Canyon? One exclaimed in amazement, "Gosh! What a hole!" And the other in equal amazement said reverently, "Stand still, and consider the wondrous works of God!" (Job 37:14)

Our words to God scattered through these pages are meant to be suggestive of types of prayers—to provide for us a language in which our own innermost feelings and aspirations may find expression, and in some instances to provide words which we may adopt as our own because they so satisfactorily express our deepest thoughts and desires.

PART I
OUR WORDS
TO ONE
ANOTHER

HOW UTTERLY AMAZING IT IS TO REALIZE HOW LARGE A proportion of our time is spent in speaking, or writing, or reading, or listening to words!

Imagine for a moment the vacuum that would be created if all telephones, radios, tape recorders, television sets, newspapers, magazines, books, and incoming mail, were suddenly removed from us. How inconceivably impoverished our lives would be! How we should be cut off from all but the handful of people whose lives directly touch ours! How we should miss the inspiration of the great literature of all ages! How the growth of knowledge of all kinds would be slowed if it could be spread only by our words to one another!

That the Bible itself came into being even before the printing press had been invented, let alone before any of these modern instruments for the transmission of words, and is still available to us centuries later, is one of the sheer marvels of history. Also marvellous is its continuing influence on generation after generation of mankind living through all the drastic changes of developing civilization. No wonder countless believers today see in these facts convincing evidence of the purposeful activity of the eternal, living God!

It should not be surprising, considering the importance to us of the ability to communicate with each other, to discover that the Bible has a great deal to say about words.

BABEL—AND PENTECOST

Two contrasting stories in the Bible, one in the Old Testament and one in the New, come to mind the moment the question is raised: "What does the Bible say about 'words'?"

The first is the story of the Tower of Babel:

And the whole earth was of one language, and of one speech.

And it came to pass, as they journeyed from the east, that they found a plain in the land of Shinar; and they dwelt there.

And they said one to another, Go to, let us make brick, and burn them thoroughly. And they had brick for stone, and slime had they for mortar.

And they said, Go to, let us build us a city and a tower, whose top may reach unto heaven; and let us make us a name, lest we be scattered abroad upon the face of the whole earth.

And the Lord came down to see the city and the tower, which the children of men builded.

And the Lord said, Behold, the people is one, and they have all one language; and this they begin to do: and now nothing will be restrained from them, which they have imagined to do.

Go to, let us go down, and there confound their language, that they may not understand one another's speech.

So the Lord scattered them abroad from thence upon the face of all the earth: and they left off to build the city.

Therefore is the name of it called Babel; because the Lord did there confound the language of all the earth.

GENESIS 11:1-9

The Tower of Babel—that monument to man's pride and arrogant self-confidence! "Let us build us a city and a tower, whose top may reach unto heaven"!

But pride can never storm the gates of heaven; only the truly humble may discover its secrets. God, the giver of the miracle of words, upset the ambitious plans of prideful men by the simple device of confounding their speech. Without the understanding of words, they could neither communicate nor work together. They were scattered abroad upon all the face of the earth.

Thousands of years later, a second, contrasting miracle is recorded. It occurred in the days following the crucifixion and the resurrection of Jesus. It was necessary for the fulfillment of God's plan that men of diverse languages *should understand each other,* and so the miracle of Pentecost and "speaking in tongues" occurred:

And when the day of Pentecost was fully come, they were all with one accord in one place.

And suddenly there came a sound from heaven as of a rushing mighty wind, and it filled all the house where they were sitting.

And there appeared unto them cloven tongues like as of fire, and it sat upon each of them.

And they were all filled with the Holy Ghost, and began to speak with other tongues, as the Spirit gave them utterance.

And there were dwelling at Jerusalem Jews, devout men, out of every nation under heaven.

Now when this was noised abroad, the multitude came together, and were confounded, because that every man heard them speak in his own language.

And they were all amazed and marvelled, saying one to another, Behold, are not all these which speak Galilaeans?

And how hear we every man in our own tongue, wherein we were born?

Parthians, and Medes, and Elamites, and the dwellers in Mesopotamia, and in Judaea, and Cappadocia, in Pontus, and Asia,

Phrygia, and Pamphylia, in Egypt, and in the parts of Libya about Cyrene, and strangers of Rome, Jews and proselytes,

Cretes and Arabians, we do hear them speak in our tongues the wonderful works of God.

And they were all amazed, and were in doubt, saying one to another, What meaneth this?

ACTS 2:1-12

Two contrasting stories of "word miracles," both pointing to the same truth: that the God-given miracle of words is to be used (as is every gift from the Creator) only for the furtherance of his eternal purposes.

OUR USE OF WORDS
FOR GOD'S PURPOSES

Why did God in his infinite wisdom endow us, his creatures, with this miraculous power of communication? If we search the scriptures a number of reasons are revealed—ways in which our use of God's gift of words may further his redemptive purpose for all mankind.

1.   Words were given us in order that we may offer thanksgiving and praise to God.

Praise ye the Lord. . . . Let every thing that hath breath praise the Lord. Praise ye the Lord.

PSALMS 150:1,6

Let us offer the sacrifice of praise to God continually, that is, the fruit of our lips giving thanks to his name.

HEBREWS 13:15

In every thing give thanks: for this is the will of God in Christ Jesus concerning you.

I THESSALONIANS 5:18

2. Words were given us that we may more clearly reveal God's truth.

The Lord God hath given me the tongue of the learned, that I should know how to speak a word in season to him that is weary: . . . he wakeneth mine ear to hear as the learned.

ISAIAH 50:4

Have not I written to thee excellent things in counsels and knowledge,

That I might make thee know the certainty of the words of truth; that thou mightest answer the words of truth to them that send unto thee?

PROVERBS 22:20-21

God will have all men to be saved, and to come unto the knowledge of the truth.

I TIMOTHY 2:4

Speak every man truth with his neighbour.

EPHESIANS 4:25

3. Words were given us to use for the edification (building up) of each other.

God hath not appointed us to wrath, but to obtain salvation by our Lord Jesus Christ.

Who died for us, that, whether we wake or sleep, we should live together with him.

Wherefore comfort yourselves together, and edify one another.

I THESSALONIANS 5:9-11

Let no corrupt communication proceed out of your mouth, but that which is good to the use of edifying, that it may minister grace unto the hearers.

EPHESIANS 4:29

4.   Words were given to us to use for the strengthening of the weak.

Behold, thou hast instructed many, and thou hast strengthened the weak hands.

Thy words have upholden him that was falling, and thou hast strengthened the feeble knees.

JOB 4:3-4

Strengthen ye the weak hands, and confirm the feeble knees.

Say to them that are of a fearful heart, Be strong, fear not: behold, your God will come . . . and save you.

ISAIAH 35:3-4

5.   Words were given to us that we may comfort the sorrowful.

Blessed be God, even the Father of our Lord Jesus Christ, the Father of mercies, and the God of all comfort;

Who comforteth us in all our tribulation, that we may be able to comfort them which are in any trouble, by the comfort wherewith we ourselves are comforted of God.

II CORINTHIANS 1:3-4

6. Words were given to us that we may be witnesses for Christ Jesus. Jesus said:

Ye shall receive power, after that the Holy Ghost is come upon you: and ye shall be witnesses unto me both in Jerusalem, and in all Judaea, and in Samaria, and unto the uttermost part of the earth.

ACTS 1:8

[Paul said:] Having therefore obtained help of God, I continue unto this day, witnessing both to small and great, saying none other things than those which the prophets and Moses did say should come.

That Christ should suffer, and that he should be the first that should rise from the dead, and should show light unto the people, and to the Gentiles.

ACTS 26:22-23

The twelve disciples and other first century Christians were not the only ones called to be witnesses for Christ. The words in Ephesians are also addressed to us, his followers today:

Unto every one of us is given grace according to the measure of the gift of Christ....

And he gave some, apostles; and some, prophets; and some, evangelists; and some, pastors and teachers;

For the perfecting of the saints, for the work of the ministry, for the edifying of the body of Christ:

Till we all come in the unity of the faith, and of the knowledge of the Son of God, unto a perfect man, unto the measure of the stature of the fulness of Christ:

That we henceforth be no more children, tossed to and fro, and carried about with every wind of doctrine....

But speaking the truth in love, may grow up into him in all things, which is the head, even Christ.

EPHESIANS 4:7,11-15

If this consideration of the use of God's gift of words for his eternal purposes has aroused in us a deeper sense of its wonder and mystery, of its potential as a redeeming force in our lives and in the lives of others, and a clearer recognition of our responsibility in the use of this gift, then we may echo with deep humility and sincerity the prayer of the psalmist:

Let the words of my mouth, and the meditation of my heart, be acceptable in thy sight, O Lord, my strength and my redeemer.

PSALMS 19:14

UNCLEAN LIPS

Although the Bible recognizes the beneficent power of words rightly used, it is realistic in its appraisal of man's usual sinfulness in this area. One evidence of this is to be found in the story of Isaiah's call to be a prophet.

In the year that king Uzziah died I saw also the Lord sitting upon a throne, high and lifted up, and his train filled the temple.

Above it stood the seraphims: each one had six wings, with twain he covered his face, and with twain he covered his feet, and with twain he did fly.

And one cried unto another, and said, Holy, holy, holy, is the Lord of hosts: the whole earth is full of his glory.

And the posts of the door moved at the voice of him that cried, and the house was filled with smoke.

Then said I, Woe is me! for I am undone; because I am a man of unclean lips, and I dwell in the midst of a people of unclean lips: for mine eyes have seen the King, the Lord of hosts.

ISAIAH 6:1-5

So to Isaiah, the vision of God's holiness was like a brilliant light, illuminating all the dark corners of his mind and revealing to him suddenly the uncleanness of his lips, and of the lips of the people in whose midst he dwelt.

Does that seem to us at first thought a small sin? A relatively unimportant one? If so, it may be that our understanding of "unclean lips" is limited. The Bible specifies a number of ways in which lips may be unclean.

In listing seven things which are "an abomination to the Lord," the writer of Proverbs mentions four that could be considered sins of unclean lips:

. . . a lying tongue, . . . an heart that deviseth wicked imaginations, . . . a false witness that speaketh lies, and he that soweth discord among brethren.

PROVERBS 6:16-19

Sins of unclean lips are recognized as characteristic of "the wicked":

The wicked, through the pride of his countenance, will not seek after God: God is not in all his thoughts.

His ways are always grievous;thy judgments are far above out of his sight. . . .

His mouth is full of cursing and deceit and fraud; under his tongue is mischief and vanity.

PSALMS 10:4-5,7

I. TWO OF THE TEN COMMANDMENTS

Of the ten basic commandments given to Moses on Mt. Sinai,

two deal specifically with our use of words. The first one is:

Thou shalt not take the name of the Lord thy God in vain; for the Lord will not hold him guiltless that taketh his name in vain.

EXODUS 20:7

In *Foundations for Reconstruction,** Dr. Elton Trueblood made some thought-provoking comments on what it means "to take the name of the Lord in vain."

> *The worst blasphemy is not profanity, but lip service. . . .*
>
> What is dangerous is not intellectual atheism . . . but the acceptance of the Judeo-Christian faith in an *attenuated and meaningless form.* And this is to take God's name in vain. It is to give lip service to moral standards, but not to take them seriously. The sin lies not in rejecting God's name, but in taking His name, *without a sense of conviction and urgency. . . .*
>
> Jesus . . . directed his strongest censure, not against the avowed pagans or infidels of his day, but against those who claimed to be believers. He made it plain that to say "Lord, Lord," has no value at all, if those who use the words do not take seriously what he said.

(Pages 31-33)

The second of the ten commandments having to do with words is:

---

*New York: Harper & Row, 1948.

Thou shalt not bear false witness against thy neighbour.

EXODUS 20:16

This commandment against false witness is repeated over and over.

Be not a witness against thy neighbour without cause; and deceive not with thy lips.

PROVERBS 24:28

A faithful witness will not lie: but a false witness will utter lies.

PROVERBS 14:5

A man that beareth false witness against his neighbour is a maul, and a sword, and a sharp arrow.

PROVERBS 25:18

A true witness delivereth souls: but a deceitful witness speaketh lies.

PROVERBS 14:25

II. LYING

Over and over again the Bible cries out against the particular sin of lying:

Lying lips are abomination to the Lord: but they that deal truly are his delight.

PROVERBS 12:22

He that hideth hatred with lying lips, and he that uttereth a slander, is a fool.

PROVERBS 10:18

Why boastest thou thyself in mischief, O mighty man? the goodness of God endureth continually.

Thy tongue deviseth mischiefs; like a sharp razor, working deceitfully.

Thou lovest evil more than good; and lying rather than to speak righteousness.

Thou lovest all devouring words, O thou deceitful tongue.

PSALMS 52:1-4

They bend their tongues like their bow for lies; but they are not valiant for the truth upon the earth; for they proceed from evil to evil, and they know not me, saith the Lord. . . .

And they will deceive every one his neighbour, and will not speak the truth: they have taught their tongue to speak lies, . . .

Their tongue is as an arrow shot out; it speaketh deceit: one speaketh peaceably to his neighbour with his mouth, but in heart he layeth his wait.

JEREMIAH 9:3,5,8

III. TALEBEARING

Had you recognized talebearing as a sin of unclean lips? The Bible speaks in no uncertain terms about it.

Thou shalt not go up and down as a talebearer among thy people.

LEVITICUS 19:16

A talebearer revealeth secrets: but he that is of a faithful spirit concealeth the matter.

PROVERBS 11:13

Thou givest thy mouth to evil, and thy tongue frameth deceit.

Thou sittest and speakest against thy brother; thou slanderest thine own mother's son.

PSALMS 50:19-20

The words of a talebearer are as wounds, and they go down into the innermost parts.

PROVERBS 18:8

Where no wood is, there the fire goeth out: so where there is no talebearer, the strife ceaseth.

PROVERBS 26:20

IV. ANGER

As might be expected, angry words are denounced in the Bible as the evil they are:

A wise man feareth and departeth from evil; but the fool rageth, and is confident.

He that is soon angry dealeth foolishly: and a man of wicked devices is hated.

PROVERBS 14:16-17

He that is slow to wrath is of great understanding: but he that is hasty of spirit exalteth folly.

PROVERBS 14:29

A soft answer turneth away wrath: but grievous words stir up anger.

PROVERBS 15:1

He that is slow to anger is better than the mighty; and he that ruleth his spirit than he that taketh a city.

PROVERBS 16:32

Make no friendship with an angry man; and with a furious man thou shalt not go:

Lest thou learn his ways, and get a snare to thy soul.

PROVERBS 22:24-25

An angry man stirreth up strife, and a furious man aboundeth in transgression.

PROVERBS 29:22

An ungodly man diggeth up evil: and in his lips there is as a burning fire.

PROVERBS 16:27

Be not hasty in thy spirit to be angry: for anger resteth in the bosom of fools.

ECCLESIASTES 7:9

DEFILEMENT

The New Testament also has much teaching about the power of words, and the abuse of that power. Remembering the Old Testament emphasis on unclean lips, Jesus' comments on what defiles a man are interesting.

Do you remember the time when some of the scribes and Pharisees from Jerusalem complained to him that his disciples did not wash their hands before eating as the tradition of the elders required? And Jesus called the multitude together and said:

Hear, and understand:

Not that which goeth into the mouth defileth a man; but that which cometh out of the mouth, this defileth a man. . . .

Those things which proceed out of the mouth come forth from the heart; and they defile the man.

For out of the heart proceed evil thoughts, murders, adulteries, fornications, thefts, false witness, blasphemies:

These are the things which defile a man.

MATTHEW 15:10-11,18-20

And again, at another time, when the Pharisees had been questioning whether his power to cast out demons was perhaps from the devil, Jesus turned upon them with these unusually harsh words:

O generation of vipers, how can ye, being evil, speak good things? for out of the abundance of the heart the mouth speaketh.

A good man out of the good treasure of the heart bringeth forth good things; and an evil man out of the evil treasure bringeth forth evil things.

But I say unto you, That every idle word that men shall speak, they shall give account thereof in the day of judgment.

For by thy words thou shalt be justified, and by thy words thou shalt be condemned.

MATTHEW 12:34-37

Paul, in his letter to the Ephesians, was rightly interpreting Jesus' teaching when he wrote:

Wherefore putting away lying, speak every man truth with his neighbour . . .

Let no corrupt communication proceed out of your mouth, but that which is good to the use of edifying, that it may minister grace unto the hearers . . .

Let all bitterness, and wrath, and anger, and clamour, and evil speaking, be put away from you, with all malice:

And be ye kind one to another, tenderhearted, forgiving one another, even as God for Christ's sake hath forgiven you.

EPHESIANS 4:25,29,31-32

Another New Testament writer, James, has given us an unforgettable picture of the power of the tongue.

If any man offend not in word, the same is a perfect man, and able also to bridle the whole body.

Behold, we put bits in the horses' mouths, that they may obey us; and we turn about their whole body.

Behold also the ships, which though they be so great, and are driven of fierce winds, yet are they turned about with a very small helm, whithersoever the governor listeth.

Even so the tongue is a little member, and boasteth great things. Behold, how great a matter a little fire kindleth!

And the tongue is a fire, a world of iniquity: so is the tongue among our members, that it defileth the whole body, and setteth on fire the course of nature; and it is set on fire of hell.

For every kind of beasts, and of birds, and of serpents, and of things in the sea, is tamed, and hath been tamed of mankind.

But the tongue can no man tame; it is an unruly evil, full of deadly poison.

Therewith bless we God, even the Father, and therewith curse we men, which are made after the similitude of God.

Out of the same mouth proceedeth blessing and cursing. My brethren, these things ought not so to be.

Doth a fountain send forth at the same place sweet water and bitter?

Can the fig tree, my brethren, bear olive berries? either a vine figs? so can no fountain both yield salt water and fresh.

Who is a wise man and endued with knowledge among you? let him show out of a good conversation his works with meekness of wisdom.

But if ye have bitter envying and strife in your hearts, glory not, and lie not against the truth.

This wisdom descendeth not from above, but is earthly, sensual, devilish.

For where envying and strife is, there is confusion and every evil work.

But the wisdom that is from above is first pure, then peaceable, gentle, and easy to be entreated, full of mercy and good fruits, without partiality, and without hypocrisy.

JAMES 3:2-17

WOE IS ME!

In the account of the Israelites in the wilderness we read:

And when the people complained, it displeased the Lord.

NUMBERS 11:1

And still does! Perhaps there is no more common sin of our lips than murmuring and complaining against the circumstances of our lives. We can see ourselves in the Israelites:

And the whole congregation of the children of Israel murmured against Moses and Aaron in the wilderness:

And the children of Israel said unto them, Would to God we had died by the hand of the Lord in the land of Egypt, when we sat by the flesh pots, and when we did eat bread to the full, for ye have brought us forth into this wilderness, to kill this whole assembly with hunger . . .

And Moses said . . . the Lord heareth your murmurings which ye murmur against him: and what are we? your murmurings are not against us, but against the Lord.

EXODUS 16:2-3,8

Murmurings and complainings almost always have their roots in a deep sense of self-pity. The word itself does not occur in the Bible, but a number of instances of its reality (in addition to the complaining Israelites) can be discovered between the lines.

Consider Elijah. After his confrontation with the prophets of Baal on Mt. Carmel (I Kings 18), he fled for his life from the wrath of Queen Jezebel.

He came after forty days and forty nights to Mt. Horeb.

And he came thither unto a cave, and lodged there; and, behold, the word of the Lord came to him, and he said unto him, What doest thou here, Elijah?

And he said, I have been very jealous for the Lord God of hosts: for the children of Israel have forsaken thy covenant, thrown down thine altars, and slain thy prophets with the sword; and I, even I only, am left; and they seek my life, to take it away.

I KINGS 19:9-10

A clear case of self-pity! And God's answer dealt positively with all excuses.

Go, return on thy way . . .

Yet I have left me seven thousand in Israel, all the knees which have not bowed unto Baal.

I KINGS 19:15,18

Consider now King Saul.

When Saul heard that David was discovered, and the men that were with him, (now Saul abode in Gibeah under a tree in Ramah, having his spear in his hand, and all his servants were standing about him;)

Then Saul said unto his servants that stood about him, Hear now, ye Benjamites, will the son of Jesse give every one of you fields and vineyards, and make you all captains of thousands, and captains of hundreds;

That all of you have conspired against me, and there is none that showeth me that my son hath made a league with the son of Jesse, and there is none of you that is sorry for me?

I SAMUEL 22:6-8

And that day, Saul's complaining and sick self-pity led to the tragic slaughter of "fourscore and five" of the priests of God.

Consider now the elder brother in Jesus' familiar parable of the prodigal son. You remember that he had not been at home when his younger brother returned, in penitence, and was welcomed by the father.

Now his elder son was in the field; and as he came and drew nigh to the house, he heard music and dancing.

And he called one of the servants, and asked what these things meant.

And he said unto him, Thy brother is come; and thy father hath killed the fatted calf, because he hath received him safe and sound.

And he was angry, and would not go in: therefore came his father out, and entreated him.

And he answering said to his father, Lo, these many years do I serve thee, neither transgressed I at any time thy commandment: and yet thou never gavest me a kid, that I might make merry with my friends:

But as soon as this thy son was come, which hath devoured thy living with harlots, thou hast killed for him the fatted calf.

LUKE 15:25-30

This last story hits near home. It is in the close personal relationships of family and intimate friends that most of us find ourselves beset by feelings of self-pity.

Innumerable other instances of complainings, murmurings and self-pity could probably be discovered in the Bible pages. These are sufficient to remind us of danger—to put us on guard against the "Woe is me!" attitude.

How do we get rid of feelings of self-pity? Fighting against them, making resolutions that we will *not* indulge in them, is rarely if ever an effective way of overcoming them. Fighting *against* these feelings often seems to root them more firmly in our minds. At the very time we are saying, "I will *not* be sorry for myself," we are actually still focussing our minds on the negative mood.

When self-pity invades our spirit, we need to hear, as did Elijah, God's challenge: "What doest thou here?" We need to take another look at the situation—an honest look free from the distortion caused by self-centeredness. We need to remind ourselves of the manifold goodness of God. This is a time to follow the psalmist's advice:

Bless the Lord, O my soul: and all that is within me, bless his holy name.

Bless the Lord, O my soul, and forget not all his benefits:

Who forgiveth all thine iniquities; who healeth all thy diseases;

Who redeemeth thy life from destruction; who crowneth thee with lovingkindness and tender mercies;

Who satisfieth thy mouth with good things . . .

Bless the Lord, O my soul.

PSALMS 103:1-5,22

Probably the most effective way to counteract self-pity and the complaining spirit is to strive to follow Paul's advice:

Let this mind be in you, which was also in Christ Jesus.

PHILIPPIANS 2:5

If we have the mind of Christ it will be an outward looking, not an inward turned, mind. It will be a mind focussed on God, not on self; seeking opportunities of service, not self-gratification. It will be a mind so open to the guidance of the indwelling Holy Spirit, so filled with awareness of God's reality and presence, that every thought of self will be crowded out.

We need to pray with deep earnestness:

Let this mind be *in me* that was in Christ Jesus.

MISCELLANEOUS BIBLE VERSES ABOUT WORDS

Some of the wise statements about words scattered through the Bible are difficult to classify, but are worth our pondering:

Help, Lord, for the godly man ceaseth; for the faithful fail from among the children of men.

They speak vanity every one with his neighbour: with flattering lips and with a double heart do they speak.

The Lord shall cut off all flattering lips, and the tongue that speaketh proud things;

Who have said, With our tongues will we prevail; our lips are our own: who is lord over us?

PSALMS 12:1-4

Lord, who shall abide in thy tabernacle? who shall dwell in thy holy hill?

He that walketh uprightly, and worketh righteousness, and speaketh the truth in his heart.

He that backbiteth not with his tongue, nor doeth evil to his neighbour, nor taketh up a reproach against his neighbour . . .

He that sweareth to his own hurt, and changeth not. . . .

He that doeth these things shall never be moved.

PSALMS 15

Keep thy tongue from evil, and thy lips from speaking guile.

PSALMS 34:13

The mouth of the righteous speaketh wisdom, and his tongue talketh of judgment.

PSALMS 37:30

The heart of the wise teacheth his mouth, and addeth learning to his lips.

Pleasant words are as an honeycomb, sweet to the soul, and health to the bones.

PROVERBS 16:23-24

Some of the proverbs are expressed in contrasting descriptive phrases.

The tongue of the wise useth knowledge aright: but the mouth of fools poureth out foolishness.

A wholesome tongue is a tree of life: but perverseness therein is a breach of the spirit.

PROVERBS 15:2,4

The thoughts of the wicked are an abomination to the Lord: but the words of the pure are pleasant words.

PROVERBS 15:26

The tongue of the just is as choice silver: the heart of the wicked is little worth.

The lips of the righteous feed many: but fools die for want of wisdom.

PROVERBS 10:20-21

Some of the proverbs are full of a sly humor. It is easy to picture the wise men sitting in the gates of the city, chuckling to one another as they observed instances of behavior that drew forth these comments:

He that hath knowledge spareth his words: . . .

Even a fool, when he holdeth his peace, is counted wise: and he that shutteth his lips is esteemed a man of understanding.

PROVERBS 17:27-28

Whoso keepeth his mouth and his tongue keepeth his soul from troubles.

PROVERBS 21:23

It is better to dwell in the corner of the housetop, than with a brawling woman in a wide house.

PROVERBS 25:24

In the multitude of words there wanteth not sin: but he that refraineth his lips is wise.

PROVERBS 10:19

Isaiah proclaims in ringing terms his unshakable faith in God's power to save, and also his understanding of the effect of sin in separating us from God's salvation:

Behold, the Lord's hand is not shortened, that it cannot save; neither his ear heavy, that it cannot hear:

But your iniquities have separated between you and your God, and your sins have hid his face from you, that he will not hear.

For your hands are defiled with blood, and your fingers with iniquity; your lips have spoken lies, your tongue hath muttered perverseness.

None calleth for justice, nor any pleadeth for truth: they trust in vanity, and speak lies; they conceive mischief, and bring forth iniquity.

ISAIAH 59:1-4

In the New Testament, Paul exhorts the early Christians to:

. . . put off all these; anger, wrath, malice, blasphemy, filthy communication out of your mouth.

Lie not one to another.

COLOSSIANS 3:8-9

One last selection: Job's forceful declaration of his mastery over his lips and tongue is one we might well make our own:

As God liveth . . . all the while my breath is in me, and the spirit of God is in my nostrils;

My lips shall not speak wickedness, nor my tongue utter deceit.

JOB 27:2-4

PRAYERS FOR THE CONTROL OF WORDS

What a keen insight the writer of Proverbs expressed when he wrote:

Death and life are in the power of the tongue.

PROVERBS 18:21

Each of us has known the two experiences suggested by these words. We have known counselors who "minister death" to us; whose words depress us, who undermine our faith in God, and our belief in ourselves, who strengthen our fears and anxieties, who reinforce all our weaknesses, who leave us worse off than we were before. But, praise God, we have also known those who "minister life"; who share with us their own buoyant faith, who affirm the best in us, who fill us with fresh confidence and joy, who leave us uplifted, strengthened, renewed, full of courage, in touch with the eternal and inexhaustible source of faith, hope and love, the Father of our Lord and Saviour, Jesus Christ.

Knowing from our own experience this power of the tongue for death or life, how earnestly we should pray that God will grant us control of our words that, in whatever situation we may find ourselves, we shall be enabled to minister life.

O Lord, attend unto my cry, give ear unto my prayer, that goeth not out of feigned lips. . . . I am purposed that my mouth shall not transgress.

PSALMS 17:1,3

Let the words of my mouth, and the meditation of my heart, be acceptable in thy sight, O Lord, my strength, and my redeemer.

PSALMS 19:14

O Lord, thou art my God. . . .

Let the lying lips be put to silence; which speak grievous things proudly and contemptuously against the righteous.

Oh how great is thy goodness, which thou hast laid up for them that fear thee; which thou hast wrought for them that trust in thee before the sons of men!

Thou shalt hide them in the secret of thy presence from the pride of man: thou shalt keep them secretly in a pavilion from the strife of tongues.

PSALMS 31:14,18-20

Remove from me the way of lying . . . I have chosen the way of truth.

PSALMS 119:29,30

[O Lord]: I will take heed to my ways, that I sin not with my

tongue: I will keep my mouth with a bridle.

PSALMS 39:1

O Lord, thou hast searched me, and known me . . .

There is not a word in my tongue, but, lo, O Lord, thou knowest it altogether. . . .

Search me, O God, and know my heart: try me, and know my thoughts:

And see if there be any wicked way in me, and lead me in the way everlasting.

PSALMS 139:1,4,23-24

Deliver my soul, O Lord, from lying lips, and from a deceitful tongue.

PSALMS 120:2

Set a watch, O Lord, before my mouth; keep the door of my lips.

PSALMS 141:3

O Lord, open thou my lips; and my mouth shall show forth thy praise.

PSALMS 51:15

May this mind be in me that was in Christ Jesus.

SEE: PHILIPPIANS 2:5

PART II
MY WORDS
TO
MYSELF

MOST OF US CARRY ON A FAIRLY STEADY AND CONTINUOUS conversation with ourselves. Until it is called to our attention, we may not be aware of it. Once you start to listen to it, however, it can reveal some surprising things about you. Moreover *until* you become aware of it, it is practically uncontrolled and uncensored. This is a dangerous situation, because out of the words you say to yourself come many of your subsequent actions.

You are driving along in your car, and *Part-of-you* is making comments to the *Rest-of-you.* "Lovely garden there." "More traffic than usual this time of day." "Looks as if it's getting ready to rain." Much of this one-sided conversation is the result of your five senses dutifully reporting, to the receiving you, all of the impressions coming their way. This is fine, and absolutely necessary for survival: you could not drive a car safely two minutes without it.

Even while you are listening to the reports of your senses, however, another conversation may well be taking place. You may be going to a meeting, and you may be talking to yourself like this:

Part-of-you: I do hope Sally isn't coming today. She is the most exasperating person! She's always against everything that's proposed.

Or you may be looking back instead of ahead, and something like this may be going on:

Part-of-you: I wonder what was the matter with Mary yesterday when she wouldn't talk to me?
Rest-of-you: Oh, what difference does it make! You don't like her anyway.

Part-of-you: I sure don't! I wish I could tell her what I really think of her.

Rest-of-you: There'll be a chance someday. And boy, will you tell her off !

Sometimes the conversation may be like this:

Part-of-you: I *wish* I didn't have to go to ——— (school, church, work, party, or ———).

Rest-of-you: You always have a rotten time.

Part-of-you: Nobody likes me at all.

Rest-of-you: That's because you're so ugly, and your clothes are never right.

Part-of-you: And I don't like *them* either. I don't care whether they like me or not. But I wish I didn't have to go.

Or again:

Part-of-you: I shouldn't have done that. What in the world made me do it?

Rest-of-you: You sure pulled a boner that time. How stupid can you be?

Or again:

Part-of-you: I'm so frightened! I'm in a real panic.

Rest-of-you: You're just a no-good coward. A 'fraidy-cat, that's you.

Part-of-you: I can't help it. I try not to be afraid.

Rest-of-you: You'll never get over it. That's the way you're made. You're just a scared rabbit.

Sometimes these almost subconscious conversations have vicious consequences. The Bible reveals an important truth when it says that as a man

. . . thinketh in his heart, so is he.

PROVERBS 23:7

Probably every criminal act that was ever committed had its origin in some similar mental exchange. Countless negative impulses have been reinforced and nourished in this way. Innumerable feeble efforts to change and improve situations have been stifled and utterly crushed by these inner conversations.

Suppose, now, that your eternal, spiritual self were to be constantly alert to what is going on within you. Suppose *this you* took control of your carnal self, to resist the evil suggestions, and to inject "the mind of Christ" into each particular situation. Something like the following might transpire:

Your Carnal Self: I do hope Sally isn't coming today. (Etc.)
Your Spiritual Self: Praise God for Sally! Every group needs one member like that. She makes us take a second look at every decision we make.

Or:

Your Carnal Self: I wonder what was the matter with Mary yesterday when she wouldn't talk to me? (Etc.)
Your Spiritual Self: But Mary is one of God's children too. He loves her just as much as he loves you. He's expecting you to love her too, no matter how difficult she is.

Or:

Your Carnal Self: I wish I didn't have to go . . . (etc.)
Your Spiritual Self: Whether people like you or not isn't important. *God loves you.* He made you and he doesn't make mistakes. You're going where he wants you to be. Just be sure you meet these people with love in your heart and everything will be all right.

Or:

Your Carnal Self: I'm so frightened! (Etc.)
Your Spiritual Self:

Wait on the Lord: be of good courage, and he shall strengthen thine heart: wait, I say, on the Lord.

PSALMS 27:14

Many times our words to ourselves will lead into words to God, and we shall find ourselves learning what it means to

Pray without ceasing.

I THESSALONIANS 5:17

As might be expected, the Bible has a good deal to say about these inner conversations. Many of the writers were deeply aware of the dangers of our words to ourselves.
Consider, for instance, this passage:

The wicked, through the pride of his countenance, will not seek after God: God is not in all his thoughts. . . .

He hath said in his heart, I shall not be moved: for I shall never be in adversity. . . .

He hath said in his heart, God hath forgotten: he hideth his face, he will never see it. . . .

. . . he hath said in his heart, Thou wilt not require it.

Thou hast seen it; for thou beholdest mischief and spite, to requite it with thy hand.

PSALMS 10:4-14

In another place, the psalmist remarks, tersely:

The fool hath said in his heart, There is no God.

PSALMS 14:1

Isaiah, prophesying against "the multitude of . . . sorceries" and "the great abundance of . . . enchantments," warned:

For thou hast trusted in thy wickedness: thou hast said, None seeth me. Thy wisdom and thy knowledge, it hath perverted thee: and thou hast said in thine heart, I am, and none else beside me.

Therefore shall evil come upon thee.

ISAIAH 47:10-11

Obadiah also sees pride as an evil often revealed by our words to ourselves:

The pride of thine heart hath deceived thee, thou that dwellest in the clefts of the rocks, whose habitation is high; that saith in his heart, Who shall bring me down to the ground?

Though thou exalt thyself as the eagle, and though thou set thy nest among the stars, thence will I bring thee down, saith the Lord.

OBADIAH 3-4

It is not only the negative aspects of our inner conversations with which the Bible deals. Nuggets of wisdom and helpful advice are sprinkled through its pages.

In Psalm 77, a beautiful way is described to overcome weariness and discouragement. Notice too in this passage another illustration of how frequently the right kind of talking to ourselves leads naturally into prayer.

My spirit was overwhelmed. . . .

I commune with my own heart . . .

Will the Lord cast off for ever? and will he be favourable no more?

Is his mercy clean gone for ever? doth his promise fail for evermore?

Hath God forgotten to be gracious? hath he in anger shut up his tender mercies?

And I said, . . . But I will remember the years of the right hand of the most High.

I will remember the works of the Lord: surely I will remember thy wonders of old.

I will meditate also of all thy work, and talk of thy doings. . . .

Thou art the God that doest wonders.

PSALMS 77:3,6-14

In Psalm 116 is an interesting illustration of how prayer led to an inner conversation, restoring peace and tranquility to a troubled heart:

The sorrows of death compassed me, and the pains of hell gat hold upon me: I found trouble and sorrow.

Then called I upon the name of the Lord . . .

Gracious is the Lord, and righteous: yea, our God is merciful . . .

I was brought low, and he helped me.

Return unto thy rest, O my soul; for the Lord hath dealt bountifully with thee.

PSALMS 116:3-7

Repeatedly, the psalmist reminds himself:

Praise the Lord, O my soul.

PSALMS 146:1

Bless the Lord, O my soul.

PSALMS 104:1

My soul, wait thou only upon God; for my expectation is from him.

He only is my rock and my salvation: he is my defence; I shall not be moved.

In God is my salvation and my glory: the rock of my strength and my refuge, is in God.

PSALMS 62:5-7

Perhaps the loveliest of these Old Testament passages is found in Psalm 103:

Bless the Lord, O my soul; and all that is within me, bless his holy name.

Bless the Lord, O my soul, and forget not all his benefits:

Who forgiveth all thine iniquities; who healeth all thy diseases;

Who redeemeth thy life from destruction, who crowneth thee with lovingkindness and tender mercies;

Who satisfieth thy mouth with good things; so that thy youth is renewed like the eagle's. . . .

Bless the Lord, O my soul.

PSALMS 103:1-5,22

Before concluding this section, it seems wise to include two New Testament passages, both parables from the teachings of Jesus, in which inner conversations occur:

And he said unto them, Take heed, and beware of covetousness: for a man's life consisteth not in the abundance of the things which he possesseth.

And he spake a parable unto them, saying, The ground of a certain rich man brought forth plentifully:

And he thought within himself, saying, What shall I do, because I have no room where to bestow my fruits?

And he said, This will I do: I will pull down my barns, and build greater; and there will I bestow all my fruits and my goods.

And I will say to my soul, Soul, thou hast much goods laid up for many years; take thine ease, eat, drink, and be merry.

But God said unto him, Thou fool, this night shall thy soul be required of thee: then whose shall those things be, which thou hast provided?

So is he that layeth up treasure for himself, and is not rich toward God.

LUKE 12:15-21

The second New Testament instance of an inner conversation occurs in Jesus' story of the prodigal son, and the son's comment to himself is in interesting contrast to that of the rich fool.

The younger son has asked and received his portion of his

inheritance. He has gone off to a far country and has "wasted his substance in riotous living." And before many days, he "began to be in want":

And he went and joined himself to a citizen of that country; and he sent him into his fields to feed swine.

And he would fain have filled his belly with the husks that the swine did eat: and no man gave unto him.

And when he came to himself, he said, How many hired servants of my father's have bread enough and to spare, and I perish with hunger!

I will arise and go to my father, and will say unto him, Father, I have sinned against heaven, and before thee,

And am no more worthy to be called thy son: make me as one of thy hired servants.

And he arose, and came to his father. But when he was yet a great way off, his father saw him, and had compassion, and ran, and fell on his neck, and kissed him.

LUKE 15:15-20

In the first parable, the rich man's words to himself "minister death." They feed his carnal self-centeredness and his reliance on himself instead of on God. In the second parable, the younger son's words to himself "minister life." They are words of wholesome confession of wrongdoing; they indicate genuine repentance; and they foreshadow positive action—return to "the Father's house."

One of the disturbing and almost unavoidable results of our paying attention to the words of our carnal selves, is that we find ourselves frequently subject to moods of spiritual depression. In an immensely helpful book, D. Martyn Lloyd-Jones has this to say:

The ultimate cause of all spiritual depression is unbelief. For if it were not for unbelief even the devil could do nothing. It is because we listen to the devil instead of listening to God that we go down before him and fall before his attacks. That is why the psalmist keeps on saying to himself: "Hope thou in God for I shall yet praise him . . ."* He reminds himself of God. . . . This man turns to himself and says: "Why art thou cast down, O my soul, why art thou disquieted within me?"* He is talking to himself, he is addressing himself. . . .

I suggest that the main trouble in this whole matter of spiritual depression in a sense is this, that we allow ourself to talk to us instead of talking to ourself. . . . Have you realized that most of your unhappiness in life is due to the fact that you are listening to yourself instead of talking to yourself? . . .

Now this man's treatment was this: instead of allowing this self to talk to him, he starts talking to himself. "Why art thou cast down, O my soul?" he asks. His soul had been depressing him, crushing him. So he stands up and says: "Self, listen for a moment, I will speak to you. . . ."

You have to take yourself in hand, you have to address yourself, preach to yourself, question yourself. You must say to your soul: "Why art thou cast down?—what business have you to be disquieted?" You must turn on yourself, upbraid yourself, condemn yourself, exhort yourself, and say to yourself: "Hope thou in God"—instead of

---

* Psalm 42.

muttering in this unhappy way. And then you must go on to remind yourself of God, who God is, and what God is and what God has done, and what God has pledged Himself to do. Then having done that, on this great note: defy yourself, and defy other people, and defy the devil and the whole world, and say with this man: "I shall yet praise him for the help of his countenance, who is also the health of my countenance and my God."*

Each of us needs to remember that:

Death and life are in the power of the tongue.

PROVERBS 18:21

Each of us needs honestly to face this question: "Do my words to myself minister life or death to my spirit?" The next section of this book, "God's Words to Us," is a fine source of biblical words that minister life, to use in conversations with yourself.**

Spiritual Depression: Its Causes and Cure. D. Martyn Lloyd-Jones, pp. 20-21. Grand Rapids, Michigan: Wm. B. Eerdmans Publishing Co. 1965.

**See also the author's recent book, *Hid in My Heart: The Word of God in Times of Need.* New York, N.Y.: Seabury Press, 1974.

PART III
GOD'S WORDS
TO US

GOD'S WORD COMES TO US, HIS CHILDREN, THROUGH MANY diverse channels. It comes, first of all, through his creation. Just as we can understand much about an artist through an appreciative study of the products of his creativity, so we can discover through the created world the omnipresence and the omnipotence of its Creator. The psalmist expressed this truth in unforgettable words:

The heavens declare the glory of God; and the firmament showeth his handiwork.

Day unto day uttereth speech, and night unto night showeth knowledge.

There is no speech or language, where their voice is not heard.

Their line is gone out through all the earth, and their words to the end of the world.

PSALMS 19:1-4

The study of man, made in God's image, can also serve as a channel through which God's Word may come to us.

When I consider thy heavens, the work of thy fingers, the moon and the stars, which thou hast ordained:

What is man, that thou art mindful of him? and the son of man, that thou visitest him?

For thou hast made him a little lower than the angels, and hast crowned him with glory and honour.

PSALMS 8:3-5

The lives of the saints bear testimony to the potential goodness of people when God-led and God-inspired; just as the lives of evil-doers testify to the lostness of humanity which rejects and denies its Creator.

Wherefore seeing we also are compassed about with so great a cloud of witnesses, let us lay aside every weight, and the sin which doth so easily beset us, and let us run with patience the race that is set before us,

Looking unto Jesus the author and finisher of our faith; who for the joy that was set before him endured the cross, despising the shame, and is set down at the right hand of . . . God.

HEBREWS 12:1-2

Countless saints in every generation bear witness to a third channel through which God's guidance comes to them: the indwelling Holy Spirit. To those who have opened their hearts, and disciplined themselves to attentiveness through study and worship, God speaks clearly and unmistakably to their inner-most spirits.

[Jesus said:] I will pray the Father, and he shall give you another Comforter, that he may abide with you for ever;

Even the Spirit of truth; whom the world cannot receive, because it seeth him not, neither knoweth him; but ye know him; for he dwelleth with you, and shall be in you.

I will not leave you comfortless . . .

The Comforter, which is the Holy Ghost, whom the Father will send in my name, he shall teach you all things, and bring to your remembrance, whatsoever I have said unto you.

JOHN 14:16-18,26

God makes use of innumerable other channels through which to reveal his Word to us, and to bestow spiritual guidance, strength and courage upon us, his children. He speaks through the circumstances of our lives; through apparently casual conversations; through newspapers, radio, and television; through the lives and writings of his saints in all generations; through the tragedies and triumphs of history; through the treasures of creative art in music, painting, literature and sculpture. In all these and countless other ways God's Word is made known to us.

Our thinking here, however, will confine itself to God's Word as it comes to us through the Bible. Not without reason has the Bible come to be called "Holy Writ" or "God's Word." This amazing collection of writings has been preserved (miraculously, many believe) through all the vicissitudes of history. It has withstood the repeated attacks of skeptics and unbelievers, of cynics and agnostics, and atheists. It continues to exert a powerful influence on thousands of people even in our present "scientific" and anti-religious generation.

In it are recorded stories of beginnings: the creation of the world and of people; the beginning of sin and rebellion against God's holy will; the story of God's plan for the redemption of mankind through a chosen people (the Hebrews), through a chosen family of that people (the family of David), and finally through the chosen Messiah, born of that family—Jesus Christ, God's "Word made flesh," whose life, death and resurrection would be the means, eventually, of bringing all men into a right relationship with God and with each other.

In the Bible are recorded God's ways of dealing with men in various typical life situations; his explicit commandments for our guidance in daily living; his warnings and revelations through his prophets, his faithful promises to those who abide in his Word.

Most important of all for Christians are the four Gospel narratives of the life, death and resurrection of Jesus Christ —who provides us with the perfect revelation of God's true being, his power, his love, his forgiveness, his glorious perfection. Truly in Jesus was God's "Word made flesh."

Nor should we neglect to mention God's Word to us as it comes through the story in Acts of the early church, and through the letters of Paul and other first century Christians, and the foreshadowing of the end times in the book of Revelation.

We should not be considering what the Bible says about words if we had not already recognized the truth that the Bible is God's Word *to us*. It is, of course, many other things. It is, unbelievably, a best-seller even in a civilization largely indifferent to all religion, and frequently in active opposition to anything remotely connected with it. It is, of course, a literary masterpiece, known throughout the world. Through the efforts of the various Bible Societies, it has been made available to countless millions of the world's population in over 2,000 languages. Whole libraries of books have been (and are still being) written about it; scholars, linguists, archeologists have made it the object of exhaustive research.

The Bible itself has many interesting things to say about "God's Word." Isaiah, speaking for God, says:

For my thoughts are not your thoughts, neither are your ways my ways, saith the Lord.

For as the heavens are higher than the earth, so are my ways higher than your ways, and my thoughts than your thoughts.

For as the rain cometh down, and the snow from heaven, and returneth not thither, but watereth the earth, and maketh it bring forth and bud, that it may give seed to the sower, and bread to the eater:

So shall my word be that goeth forth out of my mouth: it shall not return unto me void, but it shall accomplish that which I please, and it shall prosper in the thing whereto I sent it.

ISAIAH 55:8-11

All flesh is grass, and all the goodliness thereof is as the flower of the field;

The grass withereth, the flower fadeth: because the spirit of the Lord bloweth upon it: surely the people is grass.

The grass withereth, the flower fadeth: but the word of our God shall stand for ever.

ISAIAH 40:6-8

The New Testament also has much to say about "God's Word."

For the word of God is quick, and powerful, and sharper than any two-edged sword, piercing even to the dividing asunder of soul and spirit, and of the joints and marrow, and is a discerner of the thoughts and intents of the heart.

HEBREWS 4:12

Seeing ye have purified your souls in obeying the truth through the Spirit unto unfeigned love of the brethren, see that ye love one another with a pure heart fervently:

Being born again, not of corruptible seed, but of incorruptible, by the word of God, which liveth and abideth for ever.

I PETER 1:22-23

We remember too, in this connection, Jesus' parable of the sower, and his interpretation of its meaning:

The seed is the word of God.

Those by the way side are they that hear; then cometh the devil, and taketh away the word out of their hearts, lest they should believe and be saved.

They on the rock are they, which, when they hear, receive the word with joy; and these have no root, which for a while believe, and in time of temptation fall away.

And that which fell among thorns are they, which, when they have heard, go forth, and are choked with cares and riches and pleasures of this life, and bring no fruit to perfection.

But that on the good ground are they, which in an honest and good heart, having heard the word, keep it, and bring forth fruit with patience.

LUKE 8:11-15

Surely we must recognize that each one of us at times is in each of the categories Jesus described, and our prayer must be that we may grow steadily in our ability to be, and steadfastly to remain, the good ground, bringing forth fruit to the glory of God.

BIBLE DIRECTIVES FOR THE STUDY OF GOD'S WORD

For you who are reading these pages, the one fact of transcending importance is that you have come to recognize the Bible as God's Word *to you.* Otherwise you probably would never have read any further than the title page.

Even with this clear recognition, considerably more than merely reading the Bible is necessary if we are to discover in its pages God's Word for us today. It is still true that "the devil can quote Scripture to his own advantage." It is possible to quote contradictory statements, taken out of context, which confuse and becloud the Biblical message.

It is interesting and helpful to discover in the Bible itself certain directives for our approach to its spiritual treasures.

1. We are to PROVE all things.

Prove all things; hold fast that which is good.

I THESSALONIANS 5:21

The ear trieth words, as the mouth tasteth meat.

JOB 34:3

It is the viewpoint of this book that Jesus Christ himself is the final and authoritative Word of God—that all Old Testament teachings are tested, and rejected or confirmed, by Jesus' revelation of God's truth in his life, death and resurrection, and by his teachings as recorded in the Gospels.

In the beginning was the Word, and the Word was with God, and the Word was God. . . .

And the Word was made flesh, and dwelt among us, (and we beheld his glory, the glory as of the only begotten of the Father,) full of grace and truth.

JOHN 1:1,14

2. *We are to READ the Word.*

Search the scriptures.

JOHN 5:39

We cannot know what God's Word to us is unless we read it.

3. *We are to HEAR the Word.*

Faith cometh by hearing, and hearing by the word of God.

ROMANS 10:17

We hear the Word when "the body of Christ" gather together for worship and Bible study. This is one reason we are instructed:

Let us hold fast the profession of our faith without wavering; (for he is faithful that promised;)

And let us consider one another to provoke unto love and to good works:

Not forsaking the assembling of ourselves together, as the manner of some is; but exhorting one another.

HEBREWS 10:23-25

4. We are to STUDY the Word.

Study to show thyself approved unto God, a workman that needeth not to be ashamed, rightly dividing the word of truth.

II TIMOTHY 2:15

5. We are to DESIRE the Word.

As newborn babies, desire the sincere milk of the word, that ye may grow thereby.

I PETER 2:2

6. We are to MEDITATE upon the Word.

Blessed is the man that walketh not in the counsel of the

ungodly, nor standeth in the way of sinners, nor sitteth in the seat of the scornful.

But his delight is in the law of the Lord; and in his law doth he meditate day and night.

PSALMS 1:1-2

7. We are to MEMORIZE the Word.

Thy word have I hid in mine heart.

PSALMS 119:11

8. We are to PRAY about the Word.

Pray that the word of the Lord may have free course, and be glorified.

II THESSALONIANS 3:1

Open thou mine eyes, that I may behold wondrous things out of thy law.

PSALMS 119:18

9. We are to EAT the Word.

Man shall not live by bread alone, but by every word of God.

LUKE 4:4

So Jesus, quoting from the sacred scriptures of his people (Deuteronomy 8:3) resisted Satan's temptation to turn stones into bread to satisfy his hunger.

Thy words were found, and I did eat them; and thy word was unto me the joy and rejoicing of my heart.

JEREMIAH 15:16

How sweet are thy words unto my taste! yea, sweeter than honey to my mouth!

PSALMS 119:103

The idea of God's Word as nourishment for our spiritual life finds expression in a number of prophetic passages. One of the loveliest is in Isaiah:

Ho, every one that thirsteth, come ye to the waters, and he that hath no money; come ye, buy, and eat; yea, come, buy wine and milk without money and without price.

Wherefore do ye spend money for that which is not bread? and your labour for that which satisfieth not? hearken diligently unto me, and eat ye that which is good, and let your soul delight itself in fatness.

Incline your ear, and come unto me: hear, and your soul shall live.

ISAIAH 55:1-3

The New Testament recognizes this ancient truth: the comparison of "bread" and the "Word" occurs in John following the miracle of the loaves and the fishes:

And Jesus said unto them, I am the bread of life; he that cometh to me shall never hunger, and he that believeth on me shall never thirst. . . .

Verily, verily, I say unto you, He that believeth on me hath everlasting life.

I am that bread of life.

Your fathers did eat manna in the wilderness, and are dead.

This is the bread which cometh down from heaven, that a man may eat thereof, and not die.

I am the living bread which came down from heaven: if any man eat of this bread, he shall live for ever.

JOHN 6:35,47-51

Paul, writing to the Corinthians, tells of Jesus' further reference to himself as the bread of life at the time of the Last Supper:

For I have received of the Lord that which also I delivered unto you, That the Lord Jesus the same night in which he was betrayed took bread:

And when he had given thanks, he brake it, and said, Take, eat: this is my body, which is broken for you: this do in remembrance of me.

After the same manner also he took the cup, when he had supped, saying, This cup is the new testament in my blood: this do ye, as oft as ye drink it, in remembrance of me.

For as often as ye eat this bread, and drink this cup, ye do show the Lord's death till he come.

I CORINTHIANS 11:23-26

10. We are to CONTINUE OUR STUDY of the Word.

Our physical bodies are so created that they require for their well-being nourishing food in a continuous supply. Our spiritual well-being also depends on continuous feeding upon God's Word. In writing to young Timothy, Paul admonishes him:

Continue thou in the things which thou hast learned and hast been assured of, knowing of whom thou hast learned them;

And that from a child thou hast known the holy scriptures, which are able to make thee wise unto salvation through faith which is in Christ Jesus.

All scripture is given by inspiration of God, and is profitable for doctrine, for reproof, for correction, for instruction in righteousness:

That the man of God may be perfect, thoroughly furnished unto all good works.

II TIMOTHY 3:14-17

One way of encouraging ourselves in this continuing study of God's Word, is by becoming a participating member of a group of people with similar aspirations and understandings. Worship in "the body of Christ" would seem to be an essential. Also extremely valuable is membership in a smaller group—a Bible study group, a prayer circle, a "house church."

If we follow these ten Biblical directives as we study God's Word to us in the Bible, we can "prove" these words of Jesus to his disciples:

The words that I speak unto you, they are spirit, and they are life.

JOHN 6:63

WHAT *ARE* GOD'S WORDS TO US IN THE BIBLE?

The answer to this question can be summed up in one word: Jesus. Everything God wants us to know about himself, about ourselves, about his claim upon us, about our relationships to each other, about life, and death, and resurrection, he has revealed to us through Jesus Christ. Nowhere has this truth been more adequately expressed, than in the inspired words of John at the beginning of his Gospel.

In the beginning was the Word, and the Word was with God, and the Word was God. . . .

And the Word was made flesh, and dwelt among us, (and we beheld his glory, the glory as of the only begotten of the Father,) full of grace and truth.

JOHN 1:1,14

But having recognized the truth that Jesus is for us God's Word made flesh, and that in him we find the final answers to all our questions, it is still helpful to explore specific words of God to us that we find repeatedly as we study the Bible.

Eight of these directive words have been selected. Each of them will be considered in a succeeding section. Each section will include relevant "Directives and Promises" from the Bible, and selected "Responses" which we hope will become our own:

Praise Ye the Lord! (PSALMS 150)

Seek Ye My Face (PSALMS 27:8)

Have Faith in God (MARK 11:22)

Obey My Voice (EXODUS 19:5)

Love the Lord Thy God (DEUTERONOMY 6:5)

Love Thy Neighbour (LEVITICUS 19:18)

Serve the Lord (DEUTERONOMY 6:13)

Rejoice! (I THESSALONIANS 5:16)

PRAISE YE THE LORD!
(PSALMS 150)

This is an admonition repeated over and over in the Bible. *Praise*—what does it mean? Why should we praise God? Our usual use of the word *praise* is limited: we think of it often as telling someone how great, or important, or wonderful we think he is. We all like this kind of praise (although we may sometimes recognize it for flattery). Often our need for the approval it represents may be a real hindrance to our having the courage to live up to our deep convictions. (As for instance, when we are in a group, and some vicious gossip is being circulated, and we refrain from protesting; or when racial prejudice is expressed and we fail to counteract it with some positive comment.)

Such an understanding of praise has little to do with the praise we offer to God. Surely the Creator of the universe, the Father of our Lord Jesus Christ, has no need for his creatures to tell him how great, or important, or wonderful he is.

It seems likely that we are admonished to praise God because of our own need—our need to remind ourselves of God's reality, of his omnipotence, of his love for us, of our total dependence on him, of our need constantly to seek his presence, and "to enjoy him forever."

Even in our human understanding of praise, there is often a depth that goes beyond the superficial recognition of superiority. We meet a friend who has been away for a period of time, and we exclaim, "Oh, how good it is to see you again! How I missed you!"

We share an experience that has moved us deeply, and we

say, "What a joy to have been with you through this!"

Someone visits us when we are going through a valley of the shadows, and we say, "You always understand."

These are all forms of praise, but we recognize a greater depth than in the casual, "How well you are looking," or similar superficial expressions.

What makes the difference? Isn't it the element of genuine love? It is easy to say pleasant things to people, but such remarks usually mean very little unless they are expressions of true and deep concern.

Similarly, our praise to God can be merely lip service—a superficial expression, with little depth or significance.

The *Random House Dictionary* defines *praise* (verb) as follows: "to offer grateful homage to God in words or song" and suggests as similar in meaning "to glorify, magnify, exalt, and honor."

Homage is defined as (1) "respect to reverence paid or rendered," and (2) "the formal public acknowledgment by which a feudal tenant or vassal declared himself to be the man or vassal of his lord, owing him fealty, and service." And "fealty" means "fidelity, faithfulness."

So our praise to God is, in its highest and truest form, homage: an acknowledgment that we are his creatures, owing him not only life itself, but fealty, faithfulness and service.

Three elements in our praise to God are not included in the dictionary definition, but are surely present in every genuine offering of praise: love, and thanksgiving, and joy. When we are truly praising God, with our hearts as well as with our lips, we are offering our grateful love for all his benefits, and we are enjoying his presence.

In Isaiah's prophecy concerning the coming of Christ, the joyousness of praise is emphasized:

The Spirit of the Lord God is upon me, because the Lord hath anointed me . . . to comfort all that mourn . . .

To give unto them beauty for ashes, the oil of joy for mourning, the garment of praise for the spirit of heaviness.

ISAIAH 61:1-3

Passages about praise in the Bible seem to divide themselves naturally into two groups: (1) those which are directives, or exhortations, *to* praise, and (2) those which are expressions *of* praise in response to our recognition of God's reality and omnipresence. A few of each are given below; some are well worth memorizing for the enrichment of our own worship. Watch in your Bible study for other lovely praise passages.

DIRECTIVES AND PROMISES

Praise ye the Lord. Praise God in his sanctuary: praise him in the firmament of his power.

Praise him for his mighty acts: praise him according to his excellent greatness.

Praise him with the sound of the trumpet: praise him with the psaltery and harp.

Praise him with the timbrel and dance: praise him with stringed instruments and organs.

Praise him upon the loud cymbals: praise him upon the high sounding cymbals.

Let everything that hath breath praise the Lord. Praise ye the Lord.

PSALMS 150

Whoso offereth praise glorifieth me: and to him that ordereth his conversation aright will I show the salvation of God.

PSALMS 50:23

Praise ye the Lord. O give thanks unto the Lord; for he is good: for his mercy endureth for ever. . . .

Who can show forth all his praise? . . .

Blessed be the Lord God of Israel from everlasting to everlasting: and let all the people say Amen. Praise ye the Lord.

PSALMS 106:1-2,48

The living, the living, he shall praise thee, as I do this day: the father to the children shall make known thy truth.

ISAIAH 38:19

Praise ye the Lord. Praise ye the Lord from the heavens: praise him in the heights.

Praise ye him, all his angels: praise ye him, all his hosts.

Praise ye him, sun and moon: praise him, all ye stars of light.

Praise him, ye heavens of heavens, and ye waters that be above the heavens.

Let them praise the name of the Lord: for he commanded, and they were created.

He hath also stablished them for ever and ever: he hath made a decree which shall not pass.

Praise the Lord from the earth, ye dragons, and all deeps:

Fire, and hail; snow, and vapour; stormy wind fulfilling his word:

Mountains, and all hills; fruitful trees, and all cedars:

Beasts, and all cattle; creeping things, and flying fowl:

Kings of the earth, and all people; princes, and all judges of the earth:

Both young men, and maidens; old men, and children:

Let them praise the name of the Lord: for his name alone is excellent: his glory is above the earth and heaven. . . .

Praise ye the Lord.

PSALMS 148

I heard a great voice of much people in heaven, saying, Alleluia, Salvation, and glory, and honour, and power, unto the Lord our God;

For true and righteous are his judgments. . . .

And a voice came out of the throne, saying, Praise our God, all ye his servants, and ye that fear him, both small and great.

And I heard as it were the voice of a great multitude, and as the voice of many waters, and as the voice of mighty thunderings, saying, Alleluia: for the Lord God omnipotent reigneth.

Let us be glad and rejoice, and give honour to him.

REVELATION 19:1-2,5-7

RESPONSES

I will praise thee, O Lord, with my whole heart; I will show forth all thy marvellous works.

I will be glad and rejoice in thee: I will sing praise to thy name, O thou most High.

PSALMS 9:1-2

I will praise the name of God with a song, and will magnify him with thanksgiving.

This also shall please the Lord better than an ox or a bullock that hath horns and hoofs.

PSALMS 69:30-31

I will praise thee, O Lord my God, with all my heart: and I will glorify thy name for evermore.

PSALMS 86:12

My mouth shall speak the praise of the Lord.

PSALMS 145:21

Thou art my God, and I will praise thee: thou art my God, I will exalt thee.

PSALMS 118:28

God be merciful unto us, and bless us: and cause his face to shine upon us;

That thy way may be known upon earth, thy saving health among all nations.

Let the people praise thee, O God; let all the people praise thee.

O let the nations be glad and sing for joy: for thou shalt judge the people righteously, and govern the nations upon earth.

Let the people praise thee, O God; let all the people praise thee.

Then shall the earth yield her increase; and God, even our own God, shall bless us.

God shall bless us; and all the ends of the earth shall fear him.

PSALMS 67

While I live will I praise the Lord: I will sing praises unto my God while I have any being.

PSALMS 146:2

O Lord, thou art my God; I will exalt thee, I will praise thy name; for thou hast done wonderful things, thy counsels of old are faithfulness and truth. . . .

For thou hast been a strength to the poor, a strength to the needy in his distress, a refuge from the storm, a shadow from the heat.

ISAIAH 25:1,4

Because thy lovingkindness is better than life, my lips shall praise thee.

PSALMS 63:3

My tongue shall speak of thy righteousness and of thy praise all the day long.

PSALMS 35:28

O Lord, open thou my lips; and my mouth shall show forth thy praise.

PSALMS 51:15

I will sing of the mercies of the Lord for ever: with my mouth will I make known thy faithfulness to all generations.

PSALMS 89:1

SEEK YE MY FACE
(PSALMS 27:8)

In all the biblical directives to "seek the Lord" there is a basic assumption that it is God himself who puts in our hearts the desire to seek him.

John puts it this way:

In this was manifested the love of God toward us, because that God sent his only begotten Son into the world, that we might live through him.

Herein is love, not that we loved God, but that he loved us, and sent his Son to be the propitiation for our sins.

We love him, because he first loved us.

I JOHN 4:9-10,19

The Old Testament, too, recognizes this personal relationship of God to us, and his "precious thoughts unto us":

O Lord, thou hast searched me, and known me.

Thou knowest my downsitting and mine uprising, thou understandest my thought afar off.

Thou compassest my path and my lying down, and art acquainted with all my ways . . .

Thou hast beset me behind and before, and laid thine hand upon me . . .

I will praise thee: for I am fearfully and wonderfully made: marvellous are thy works; and that my soul knoweth right well . . .

Thine eyes did see my substance, yet being unperfect; and in thy book all my members were written, which in continuance were fashioned, when as yet there was none of them.

How precious also are thy thoughts unto me, O God! how great is the sum of them!

If I should count them, they are more in number than the sand.

PSALMS 139:1-5, 14-18

Again, as in the preceding section, the relevant biblical passages divide themselves into two categories: the directives and promises of God, and our responses:

DIRECTIVES AND PROMISES

Seek ye the Lord while he may be found, call ye upon him while he is near.

ISAIAH 55:6

If . . . thou shalt seek the Lord thy God, thou shalt find him, if thou seek him with all thy heart and with all thy soul.

DEUTERONOMY 4:29

The hand of our God is upon all them for good that seek him.

EZRA 8:22

They that know thy name will put their trust in thee: for thou, Lord, hast not forsaken them that seek thee.

PSALMS 9:10

Ye shall seek me, and find me, when ye shall search for me with all your heart.

And I will be found of you, saith the Lord.

JEREMIAH 29:13-14

Thus saith the Lord . . . Seek ye me, and ye shall live: . . .

Seek him that maketh the seven stars and Orion, and turneth the shadow of death into the morning, and maketh the day dark with night: that calleth for the waters of the sea, and poureth them out upon the face of the earth: the Lord is his name.

AMOS 5:4,8

Ask, and it shall be given you; seek, and ye shall find; knock, and it shall be opened unto you:

For every one that asketh receiveth, and he that seeketh findeth; and to him that knocketh it shall be opened.

MATTHEW 7:7-8

RESPONSES

When thou saidst, Seek ye my face; my heart said unto thee, Thy face, Lord, will I seek.

PSALMS 27:8

With my soul have I desired thee in the night; yea, with my spirit within me will I seek thee early.

ISAIAH 26:9

I would seek unto God, and unto God would I commit my cause:

Which doeth great things and unsearchable; marvellous things without number.

JOB 5:8-9

I sought the Lord, and he heard me, and delivered me from all my fears.

PSALMS 34:4

With my whole heart have I sought thee: O let me not wander from thy commandments.

PSALMS 119:10

O God, thou art my God; early will I seek thee: my soul thirsteth for thee, my flesh longeth for thee in a dry and thirsty land, where no water is;

To see thy power and thy glory.

PSALMS 63:1-2

As the hart panteth after the water brooks, so panteth my soul after thee, O God.

My soul thirsteth for God, for the living God.

PSALMS 42:1-2

HAVE FAITH IN GOD
(MARK 11:22)

Have faith! Trust! Believe! If these words and the sentences in which they occur were deleted from our Bible, how impoverished would be our spiritual heritage!

Each one of us must sometimes echo the prayer of the father of the demon-possessed child:

Lord, I believe; help thou mine unbelief.

MARK 9:24

In Romans, Paul states:

Faith cometh by hearing, and hearing by the word of God.

ROMANS 10:17

Those of us who are desirous of increasing our faith know two sure ways of achieving our desire. One is by steady and continuous study of the Word of God. It has already been pointed out that just as the body requires daily food in order to achieve and maintain maximum efficiency, so our spiritual well-being depends upon continuous, daily spiritual nourishment.

The second way of deepening our faith is in close and frequent fellowship with spirit-filled Christians. Faith is contagious.

The nature of faith, and its importance, has been pointed out by Paul in one of the most famous passages in the Bible:

Now faith is the substance of things hoped for, the evidence of things not seen. . . .

Through faith we understand that the worlds were framed by the word of God, so that things which are seen were not made of things which do appear. . . .

Without faith it is impossible to please him [God] for he that cometh to God must believe that he is, and that he is a rewarder of them that diligently seek him.

HEBREWS 11:1,3,6

DIRECTIVES AND PROMISES

They that trust in the Lord shall be as mount Zion, which cannot be removed, but abideth for ever.

As the mountains are round about Jerusalem, so the Lord is round about his people from henceforth even for ever.

PSALMS 125:1-2

It is better to trust in the Lord than to put confidence in man.

PSALMS 118:8

Repent ye, and believe the gospel.

MARK 1:15

Trust in the Lord with all thine heart; and lean not unto thine own understanding.

In all thy ways acknowledge him, and he shall direct thy paths.

PROVERBS 3:5-6

Believe in the Lord your God, so shall ye be established; believe his prophets, so shall ye prosper.

II CHRONICLES 20:20

Trust in him at all times, ye people, pour out your heart before him: God is a refuge for us.

PSALMS 62:8

Thou wilt keep him in perfect peace, whose mind is stayed on thee: because he trusteth in thee.

Trust ye in the Lord for ever: for in the Lord Jehovah is everlasting strength.

ISAIAH 26:3-4

For God so loved the world, that he gave his only begotten Son, that whosoever believeth in him should not perish, but have everlasting life.

For God sent not his Son into the world to condemn the world; but that the world through him might be saved.

JOHN 3:16-17

[Jesus said:] Let not your heart be troubled: ye believe in God, believe also in me.

In my Father's house are many mansions: if it were not so, I would have told you. I go to prepare a place for you.

And if I go and prepare a place for you, I will come again, and receive you unto myself; that where I am, there ye may be also.

JOHN 14:1-3

RESPONSES

In God is my salvation and my glory: the rock of my strength, and my refuge, is in God.

PSALMS 62:7

Behold, God is my salvation; I will trust, and not be afraid: for the Lord Jehovah is my strength and my song: he also is become my salvation.

ISAIAH 12:2

Lord, increase our faith.

LUKE 17:5

O thou most High,
What time I am afraid, I will trust in thee. . . .
In God I have put my trust; I will not fear what flesh can do unto me.

PSALMS 56:2-4

The Lord is my light and my salvation; whom shall I fear? the Lord is the strength of my life, of whom shall I be afraid?

PSALMS 27:1

We trust in the living God, who is the Saviour of all men.

I TIMOTHY 4:10

Though he slay me, yet will I trust in him.

JOB 13:15

The Lord is my rock, and my fortress, and my deliverer; my God, my strength, in whom I will trust.

PSALMS 18:2

Hear my prayer, O Lord, give ear to my supplications: in thy faithfulness answer me, and in thy righteousness. . . .

I stretch forth my hands unto thee: my soul thirsteth after thee, as a thirsty land. . . .

Hear me speedily, O Lord: my spirit faileth: hide not thy face from me, . . .

Cause me to hear thy lovingkindness in the morning; for in thee do I trust: cause me to know the way wherein I should walk; for I lift up my soul unto thee.

PSALMS 143:1,6-8

Now, may the God of hope fill us with all joy and peace in believing, that we may abound in hope, through the power of the Holy Ghost.

SEE: ROMANS 15:13

Blessed be thou, God and Father of our Lord Jesus Christ, which according to thine abundant mercy hast begotten us again unto a lively hope by the resurrection of Jesus Christ from the dead,

To an inheritance incorruptible, and undefiled, and that fadeth not away, reserved in heaven for us,

Who are kept by thy power, God, through faith unto salvation ready to be revealed in the last time.

Wherein we greatly rejoice, though now for a season, if need be, we are in heaviness through manifold temptations:

That the trial of our faith, being much more precious than of gold that perisheth, though it be tried with fire, might be found unto praise and honour and glory at the appearing of Jesus Christ:

Whom having not seen, we love; in whom, though now we see him not, yet believing, we rejoice with joy unspeakable and full of glory.

SEE: I PETER 1:3-9

OBEY MY VOICE
(EXODUS 19:5)

1. In the Wilderness of Sinai

The commandment to obey God's voice appears in the account of the early days of the Exodus:

In the third month, when the children of Israel were gone forth out of the land of Egypt, the same day came they unto the wilderness of Sinai . . .

And the Lord called unto Moses out of the mountain, saying, Thus shalt thou . . . tell the children of Israel;*

Now therefore, if ye will obey my voice indeed, and keep my covenant, then ye shall be a peculiar [very special] treasure unto me above all people: for all the earth is mine:

And ye shall be unto me a kingdom of priests, and an holy nation.

EXODUS 19:1,3,5-6

Years later, near the end of Moses' life, he is pleading with his people once again to give God their undivided allegiance:

And the Lord thy God will circumcise thine heart, and the heart of thy seed, to love the Lord thy God with all thine heart, and with all thy soul, that thou mayest live . . .

And the Lord thy God will make thee plenteous in every work of thine hand, in the fruit of thy body, and in the fruit of thy cattle, and in the fruit of thy land, for good: for the Lord will again rejoice over thee for good . . .

If thou shalt hearken unto the voice of the Lord thy God, to keep

---

* We need to remember that we today are a part of "the children of Israel," and that promises to them are promises to us.

*his commandments . . . and if thou turn unto the Lord thy God
with all thine heart, and with all thy soul.*

*For this commandment which I command thee this day, it is not
hidden from thee, neither is it far off.*

*It is not in heaven, that thou shouldest say, Who shall go up for
us to heaven, and bring it unto us, that we may hear it, and do
it?*

*Neither is it beyond the sea, that thou shouldest say, Who shall
go over the sea for us, and bring it unto us, that we may hear it,
and do it?*

*But the word is very nigh unto thee, in thy mouth, and in thy
heart, that thou mayest do it.*

DEUTERONOMY 30:6,9-14

2. *We Cannot But Speak*
(ACTS 4:20)

A New Testament story having to do with obedience to God is
found in Acts 3, 4 and 5. This is part of the account of the
witnessing of the apostles in Jerusalem after Pentecost.

It began when Peter and John went up together to the
Temple to pray. Entering in at the "gate which is called Beautiful," they healed a man lame from his mother's womb.

This miracle drew together a crowd of people, "greatly wondering." To them, Peter preached boldly, reminding them of God's repeated promise through the prophets of a Messiah, and declaring to them that this promise had been fulfilled in Jesus.

The temple authorities, however, interrupted Peter's witnessing, arrested Peter and John, and put them in prison overnight. The next morning the two were brought before the high priest, and "a group of rulers, and elders and scribes." After being questioned, Peter and John were commanded "not to speak at all nor teach in the name of Jesus."

But Peter and John answered and said unto them, Whether it be right in the sight of God to hearken unto you more than unto God, judge ye.

For we cannot but speak the things which we have seen and heard.

So when they had further threatened them, they let them go, finding nothing how they might punish them, because of the people: for all men glorified God for that which was done.

ACTS 4:18-21

3. *Christ Learned Obedience*
(HEBREWS 5:8)

Any consideration of obedience to God leads inevitably to the darkness of night in the Garden of Gethsemane. How tremendous is the insight in Hebrews, when the writer, speaking of Jesus, says:

Though he were a Son, yet learned he obedience by the things which he suffered.

HEBREWS 5:8

The Garden of Gethsemane at night—the shadowy darkness —the flickering lights of torches—Simon Peter's impulsive act in drawing his sword, and cutting off the ear of Malchus—and then Jesus' quiet rebuke:

Put up thy sword into the sheath: the cup which my Father hath given me, shall I not drink it?

JOHN 18:11

DIRECTIVES AND PROMISES

Ye shall walk after the Lord your God, and fear* him, and keep his commandments.

DEUTERONOMY 13:4

And Samuel said, Hath the Lord as great delight in burnt offerings and sacrifices, as in obeying the voice of the Lord? Behold, to obey is better than sacrifice.

I SAMUEL 15:22

---

*Probably *revere* rather than *be afraid of.*

Thus saith the Lord God of Israel . . . Obey my voice . . . according to all which I command you: so shall ye be my people, and I will be your God.

JEREMIAH 11:3-4

The kingdom and dominion, and the greatness of the kingdom under the whole heaven, shall be given to the people of the saints of the most High, whose kingdom is an everlasting kingdom, and all dominions shall serve and obey him.

DANIEL 7:27

Is not this the fast that I have chosen? to loose the bands of wickedness, to undo the heavy burdens, and to let the oppressed go free, and that ye break every yoke?

Is it not to deal thy bread to the hungry, and that thou bring the poor that are cast out to thy house? when thou seest the naked, that thou cover him . . .?

Then shall thy light break forth as the morning, and thine health shall spring forth speedily: and thy righteousness shall go before thee; the glory of the Lord shall be thy rereward.

Then shalt thou call, and the Lord shall answer; thou shalt cry, and he shall say, Here I am.

ISAIAH 58:6-9

RESPONSES

God our Father, grant that we may have strength to cast down everything that exalteth itself against our knowledge of thee, and to bring into captivity every thought to the obedience of Christ. Amen.

SEE: II CORINTHIANS 10:5

Holy Father, as Jesus learned obedience through the things he suffered, grant that we too may learn obedience to thee from every circumstance of our lives. Amen.

SEE: HEBREWS 5:8

Teach me, O Lord, the way of thy statutes; and I shall keep it unto the end.

Give me understanding, and I shall keep thy law; yea, I shall observe it with my whole heart.

Make me to go in the path of thy commandments; for therein do I delight.

Incline my heart unto thy testimonies . . . and quicken thou me in thy way.

PSALMS 119:33-37

Help us, God our Father, to follow after righteousness, godliness, faith, love, patience, meekness: to fight the good fight of faith, and to lay hold on eternal life. Amen.

SEE: I TIMOTHY 6:11-12

All that the Lord hath said will we do, and be obedient.

EXODUS 24:7

Holy Father, when we do well, and suffer for it, help us to take it patiently, knowing that this is acceptable with thee.

For even hereunto were we called: because Christ suffered for us, leaving us an example that we should follow his steps:

Who did no sin, neither was guile found in his mouth;

Who, when he was reviled, reviled not again; when he suffered, he threatened not; but committed himself to thee who judgest righteously. Amen.

SEE: I PETER 2:20-23

LOVE THE LORD THY GOD
(DEUTERONOMY 6:5)

1. Positive and Negative Commandments

It is an over-simplification, but it still has a measure of truth: the Old Testament religion is largely a matter of a few "do's" and a great number of "don't's".

It is interesting to note that of the Ten Commandments all but two are "thou shalt not's"; and of those two, one that is stated positively (Remember the sabbath day to keep it holy) immediately goes into the negative:

But the seventh day is the sabbath of the Lord thy God: in it thou shalt not do any work, . . . [etc.]

EXODUS 20:10

There is one notable exception to the instances of negative commandments in the Old Testament:

Hear, O Israel: The Lord our God is one Lord:

And thou shalt love the Lord thy God with all thine heart, and with all thy soul, and with all thy might.

And these words, which I command thee this day, shall be in thine heart:

And thou shalt teach them diligently unto thy children, and shalt talk of them when thou sittest in thine house, and when thou walkest by the way, and when thou liest down, and when thou risest up.

DEUTERONOMY 6:4-7

There are of course other exceptions, notably in the writings of the prophets, to the prevalence of negative commandments in the Old Testament.

Amos, speaking for God, and protesting against the mere observance of rules and regulations without genuine devotion to God's will, says:

I hate, I despise your feast days, and I will not smell in your solemn assemblies.

Though ye offer me burnt offerings and your meat offerings, I will not accept them: neither will I regard the peace offerings of your fat beasts.

Take thou away from me the noise of thy songs; for I will not hear the melody of thy viols.

But let judgment run down as waters, and righteousness as a mighty stream.

AMOS 5:21-24

Micah also cries out against the uselessness of following rules unless the heart is right:

Wherewith shall I come before the Lord, and bow myself before the high God? shall I come before him with burnt offerings, with calves of a year old?

Will the Lord be pleased with thousands of rams, or with ten thousands of rivers of oil? shall I give my firstborn for my transgression, the fruit of my body for the sin of my soul?

He hath showed thee, O man, what is good; and what doth the Lord require of thee, but to do justly, and to love mercy, and to walk humbly with thy God?

MICAH 6:6-8

Hosea adds his witness that observances and legalistic customs followed without genuine dedication are of no value. As a spokesman for God, he says:

O Ephraim, what shall I do unto thee? O Judah, what shall I do unto thee? for your goodness is as a morning cloud, and as the early dew it goeth away. . . .

For I desired mercy, and not sacrifice; and the knowledge of God more than burnt offerings.

HOSEA 6:4,6

Against the legalistic ethics of his time, Jesus joined the chorus of prophetic protest. On one occasion, when the Pharisees questioned his eating with "publicans and sinners," he referred to Hosea's words:

Go ye and learn what that meaneth, I will have mercy and not sacrifice.

MATTHEW 9:13

Several times he defied the rigid rules for the sabbath observance:

And, behold, there was a man which had his hand withered. And they asked him, saying, Is it lawful to heal on the sabbath days? that they might accuse him.

And he said unto them, What man shall there be among you, that shall have one sheep. and if it fall into a pit on the sabbath day, will he not lay hold on it, and lift it out?

How much then is a man better than a sheep? Wherefore it is lawful to do well on the sabbath days.

Then saith he to the man, Stretch forth thine hand. And he stretched it forth; and it was restored whole, like as the other.

MATTHEW 12:10-13

And again, on yet another occasion, Jesus said:

The sabbath was made for man, and not man for the sabbath.

MARK 2:27

In contrast to the legalism of the Old Testament, the thrust of Jesus' teaching is a liberating, powerful, positive ethic of love.

If the two most significant passages in the Gospels were to be chosen, the two following might well be selected—one proclaiming God's love for the world, and the other emphasizing the importance of our twofold response to God's love for us, in love to God and love to our fellowmen.

For God so loved the world, that he gave his only begotten Son, that whosoever believeth in him should not perish, but have everlasting life.

JOHN 3:16

Then one of them which was a lawyer, asked him a question, tempting him, and saying,

Master, which is the great commandment in the law?

Jesus said unto him, Thou shalt love the Lord thy God with all thy heart, and with all thy soul, and with all thy mind.

This is the first and great commandment.

And the second is like unto it, Thou shalt love thy neighbour as thyself.

On these two commandments hang all the law and the prophets.

MATTHEW 22:35-40

God's love for us, and our response to that love—surely these are God's words to us through Jesus' life and teachings, through his death and resurrection.

2. God the Loving Father

When Jesus chose to put primary emphasis on the commandment to love God, he was at great pains to reveal the divine nature of the God to whom our human love was to be given.

As is true of many of Jesus' teachings, the recognition of God as the loving Father of us, his creatures, is dimly foreshadowed in the Old Testament.

Isaiah three times refers to God as "Father":

Thou, O Lord, art our father, our redeemer; thy name is from everlasting.

ISAIAH 63:16

O Lord, thou art our father; we are the clay, and thou our potter; and we all are the work of thy hand.

ISAIAH 64:8

And in the famous prophecy of the coming Messiah, he says:

Unto us a child is born, unto us a Son is given: . . . and his name shall be called . . . The everlasting Father.

ISAIAH 9:6

The psalmist also says:

A father of the fatherless . . . is God in his holy habitation.

PSALMS 68:5

Like as a father pitieth his children, so the Lord pitieth them that fear him.

PSALMS 103:13

In Proverbs we find this advice:

My son, despise not the chastening of the Lord; neither be weary of his correction:

For whom the Lord loveth he correcteth; even as a father the son in whom he delighteth.

PROVERBS 3:11-12

The prophet Malachi echoed this insight when he pleaded:

Have we not all one father? hath not one God created us? why do we deal treacherously every man against his brother?

MALACHI 2:10

It remained, however, for Jesus to take this embryonic idea of the Fatherhood of God and to show it forth in all its saving and redeeming beauty. Few of his teachings are as much loved and as frequently quoted as his parable of the prodigal son.

You remember of course what finally happened when the younger son "came to himself ":

And he arose, and came to his father. But when he was yet a great way off, his father saw him, and had compassion, and ran, and fell on his neck, and kissed him.

And the son said unto him, Father, I have sinned against heaven, and in thy sight, and am no more worthy to be called thy son.

But the father said to his servants, Bring forth the best robe, and put it on him; and put a ring on his hand, and shoes on his feet:

And bring hither the fatted calf, and kill it; and let us eat, and be merry:

For this my son was dead, and is alive again; he was lost, and is found. And they began to be merry.

LUKE 15:20-24

Over and over again, in unforgettable words and parables, Jesus repeated this basic thrust of his teaching—the unchangeable love of the Father God for the children of his creation.

No wonder John exclaims:

Behold, what manner of love the Father hath bestowed upon us, that we should be called the sons of God . . .

I JOHN 3:1

Always in Jesus' teaching this love is a free gift; never is it dependent upon our response to it. Always the loving forgiveness of God is available for the asking, and always the forgiveness is accompanied with rejoicing.

And Jesus spoke this parable unto them, saying,

What man of you, having an hundred sheep, if he lose one of them, doth not leave the ninety and nine in the wilderness, and go after that which is lost, until he find it?

And when he hath found it, he layeth it on his shoulders, rejoicing,

And when he cometh home, he calleth together his friends and neighbours, saying unto them, Rejoice with me, for I have found my sheep which was lost.

I say unto you, that likewise joy shall be in heaven over one sinner that repenteth, more than over ninety and nine just persons which need no repentance.

LUKE 15:3-7

In Jesus' sermon on the mount (Matthew 5, 6, 7) the name "Father" is applied to God seventeen times. Let us consider now what additional insights about our Father and our relationship to him Jesus is teaching in these chapters.

GOD IS GLORIFIED BY THE "GOOD WORKS" OF HIS CHILDREN. How true this is even on the human level of father-child relationships! Human parents receive reflected credit for their children's achievements and well-doing, and are "glorified" thereby.

Let your light so shine before men, that they may see your good works, and glorify your Father which is in heaven.

MATTHEW 5:16

OUR FATHER IS IMPARTIAL. His good gifts are freely provided for all his children. So we too are to express love in every relationship of our lives.

Ye have heard that it hath been said, Thou shalt love thy neighbour, and hate thine enemy.

But I say unto you, Love your enemies, bless them that curse you, do good to them that hate you, and pray for them which despitefully use you, . . .

That ye may be the children of your Father which is in heaven: for he maketh his sun to rise on the evil and on the good, and sendeth rain on the just and on the unjust.

Be ye therefore perfect, even as your Father which is in heaven is perfect.

MATTHEW 5:43-45,48

OUR FATHER KNOWS ALL THE SECRETS OF OUR HEARTS.

Take heed that you do not your alms before men, to be seen of them: otherwise ye have no reward of your Father which is in heaven.

But when thou doest alms, let not thy left hand know what thy right hand doeth:

That thine alms may be in secret: and thy Father which seeth in secret himself shall reward thee openly.

MATTHEW 6:1,3-4

GOD HEARS OUR PRAYERS. He knows our needs before we ask.

And when thou prayest, thou shalt not be as the hypocrites are . . .

But thou, when thou prayest, enter into thy closet, and when thou hast shut thy door, pray to thy Father which is in secret; and thy Father which seeth in secret shall reward thee openly.

But when ye pray, use not vain repetitions, as the heathen do; for they think that they shall be heard for their much speaking.

Be not ye therefore like unto them: for your Father knoweth what things ye have need of, before ye ask him.

MATTHEW 6:5-8

OUR FATHER IS READY TO FORGIVE US, when we ourselves forgive others.

If ye forgive men their trespasses, your Heavenly Father will also forgive you:

But if ye forgive not men their trespasses, neither will your Father forgive your trespasses.

MATTHEW 6:14-15

OUR FATHER SEES THE HIDDEN MOTIVES OF OUR HEARTS.

Thou, when thou fastest, anoint thine head, and wash thy face;

That thou appear not unto men to fast, but unto thy Father which is in secret: and thy Father which seeth in secret shall reward thee openly.

MATTHEW 6:17-18

OUR FATHER DELIGHTS TO MEET THE NEEDS OF ALL HIS CHILDREN AND TO GIVE GOOD GIFTS TO THEM.

Behold the fowls of the air: for they sow not, neither do they reap, nor gather into barns; yet your heavenly Father feedeth them. Are ye not much better than they? . . .

And why take ye thought for raiment? Consider the lilies of the field, how they grow; they toil not, neither do they spin:

And yet I say unto you, That even Solomon in all his glory was not arrayed like one of these.

Wherefore, If God so clothe the grass of the field, which today is, and tomorrow is cast into the oven, shall he not much more clothe you, O ye of little faith?

Therefore take no thought, saying, What shall we eat? or, What shall we drink? or, Wherewithal shall we be clothed? . . .

. . . for your heavenly Father knoweth that ye have need of all these things.

But seek ye first the kingdom of God, and his righteousness; and all these things shall be added unto you.

MATTHEW 6:26-33

What man is there of you, whom if his son ask bread, will he give him a stone?

If ye then, being evil, know how to give good gifts unto your children, how much more shall your Father which is in heaven give good things to them that ask him?

MATTHEW 7:9-11

OUR FATHER EXPECTS WILLING OBEDIENCE FROM HIS CHILDREN.

Not every one that saith unto me, Lord, Lord, shall enter into the kingdom of heaven: but he that doeth the will of my Father which is in heaven.

MATTHEW 7:21

SUMMARY: Jesus' teaching about the God we are commanded to love is partially contained in the following truths:

God is our loving Father. He is glorified by the good works of his children. He is impartial: his good gifts are provided for all. He knows all the secrets of our hearts. He hears our prayers. He knows our needs before we ask. He is ready to forgive us when we forgive others. He sees the hidden motives of our hearts. He delights to meet all our needs, and to give good gifts to us. He expects willing obedience from us, his children.

One of the early followers of Jesus who took to heart this assurance of God's love was Paul. Every Christian should make Paul's confession of faith his own:

Who shall separate us from the love of Christ? shall tribulation, or distress, or persecution, or famine, or nakedness, or peril or sword? . . .

Nay, in all these things we are more than conquerors through him that loved us.

For I am persuaded, that neither death, nor life, nor angels, nor principalities, nor powers, nor things present, nor things to come,

Nor height, nor depth, nor any other creature, shall be able to separate us from the love of God which is in Christ Jesus, our Lord.

ROMANS 8:35-39

DIRECTIVES AND PROMISES

We have already considered the chief directive for our love to God, the commandment:

Thou shalt love the Lord thy God with all thine heart, and with all thy soul, and with all thy might.

DEUTERONOMY 6:5

And we have recalled Jesus' choice of this as the "first and great" commandment. (Matthew 22:37) Many other directives are scattered through the pages of the Bible:

O love the Lord, all ye his saints: for the Lord preserveth the faithful.

PSALMS 31:23

The Lord preserveth all them that love him.

PSALMS 145:20

The Lord hath appeared of old unto me, saying, Yea, I have loved thee with an everlasting love; therefore with lovingkindness have I drawn thee.

JEREMIAH 31:3

We know that all things work together for good to them that love

God, to them who are the called according to his purpose.

ROMANS 8:28

Eye hath not seen, nor ear heard, neither have entered into the heart of man, the things which God hath prepared for them that love him.

I CORINTHIANS 2:9

Hearken, my beloved brethren, Hath not God chosen the poor of this world rich in faith, and heirs of the kingdom which he hath promised to them that love him?

JAMES 2:5

Blessed is the man that endureth temptation: for when he is tried, he shall receive the crown of life, which the Lord hath promised to them that love him.

JAMES 1:12

Now our Lord Jesus Christ himself, and God, even our Father, which hath loved us, and hath given us everlasting consolation and good hope through grace,

Comfort your hearts, and stablish you in every good word and work.

II THESSALONIANS 2:16-17

RESPONSES

I will love thee, O Lord, my strength.

PSALMS 18:1

I love the Lord, because he hath heard my voice and my supplications.

Because he hath inclined his ear unto me, therefore will I call upon him as long as I live.

PSALMS 116:1-2

Unto thee, O Lord, do I lift up my soul.

For thou, Lord, art good, and ready to forgive, and plenteous in mercy unto all them that call upon thee . . .

Thou art great and doest wondrous things.

PSALMS 86:4-5, 10

We have known and believed the love that God hath to us. God is love; and he that dwelleth in love dwelleth in God, and God in him. . . .

We love him, because he first loved us.

I JOHN 4:16,19

My little children, let us not love in word, neither in tongue; but in deed and in truth.

I JOHN 3:18

Beloved, if God so loved us, we ought also to love one another.

I JOHN 4:11

Grant, holy Father, according to the riches of thy glory, that I may be strengthened with might by thine indwelling Spirit;

That Christ may dwell in my heart by faith; that I being rooted and grounded in love,

May be able to comprehend with all the saints what is the breadth, and length, and depth, and height;

And to know the love of Christ which passeth knowledge, that I may be filled with all thy fulness. Amen.

SEE: EPHESIANS 3:16-19

Holy Father: Enable me to present my body a living sacrifice, holy, acceptable unto thee, which is my reasonable service.

And give me strength, I pray, not to be conformed to this world, but to be transformed by the renewing of my mind, that I may prove what is that good and acceptable, and perfect, will of thine for me. Amen.

SEE: ROMANS 12:1-2

Father: Enable me, I pray, to love with the love that suffereth long and is kind, that envieth not, that vaunteth not itself, is not puffed up,

Doth not behave itself unseemly, seeketh not her own, is not easily provoked, thinketh no evil;

That rejoiceth not in iniquity, but rejoiceth in the truth;

That beareth all things, believeth all things, hopeth all things, endureth all things.

The love that never faileth. Amen.

SEE: I CORINTHIANS 13:4-8

Heavenly Father, grant that I may be filled with the knowledge of thy will in all wisdom and spiritual understanding;

That I may walk worthy of thee, O Lord, unto all pleasing, being fruitful in every good work, and increasing in the knowledge of thee;

Strengthened with all might, according to thy glorious power, unto all patience and longsuffering with joyfulness;

Giving thanks unto thee, O Father, who hath delivered me from the power of darkness, and hath translated me into the kingdom of thy dear Son. Amen.

SEE: COLOSSIANS 1:9-13

LOVE THY NEIGHBOUR
(LEVITICUS 19: 18)

The commandment to "love God with all thine heart, and with all thy soul, and with all thy might" appears first in Deuteronomy 6:5. It is repeated with minor variations five times in the same book.*

When Jesus quoted this as the "first and great commandment" ** he linked closely with it a far less familiar one, a part of a verse in Leviticus almost buried in a list of "thou shalt nots."

Thou shalt love thy neighbour as thyself.

LEVITICUS 19:18

Those who have very slight knowledge of the New Testament are still likely to be familiar with Jesus' story of the Good Samaritan, told in answer to the question: "Who is my neighbour?" (Luke 10:25-37.)

It has been pointed out that the parable answers the question only by implication. Instead of giving a direct answer, Jesus posed a second question:

Which now of these three, thinkest thou, was neighbour unto him that fell among the thieves?

---

* Deuteronomy 10:12; 11:1, 13,22; 19:9; 30:6.
** Matthew 22:39; Mark 12:31; Luke 10:27.

And he said, He that showed mercy on him. Then said Jesus
unto him, Go, and do thou likewise.

LUKE 10:36-37

In this story, Jesus immeasurably broadened the original meaning of the commandment. In its initial form "Love thy neighbour" applied only to other Hebrews:

Thou shalt not avenge, nor bear any grudge against the children
of thy people, *but thou shalt love thy neighbour as thyself.*

LEVITICUS 19:18

Farther along in the same chapter the commandment is
broadened slightly:

The stranger that dwelleth with you shall be unto you as one
born among you, and thou shalt love him as thyself; for ye were
strangers in the land of Egypt: I am the Lord your God.

LEVITICUS 19:34

But, as in other instances, Jesus took an embryonic idea in the
Old Testament and transformed it into a challenging directive
for a life dedicated to God. Refusing to limit the definition of
"neighbour" by any qualifications, he laid upon the hearts of his
followers the claim of *anyone in need.*

That Jesus' followers took to heart his emphasis on love of
neighbours is witnessed by three references to it in the epistles:

Owe no man any thing, but to love one another: for he that
loveth another hath fulfilled the law:

For this, Thou shalt not commit adultery, Thou shalt not kill, Thou shalt not steal, Thou shalt not bear false witness, Thou shalt not covet; and if there be any other commandment, it is briefly comprehended in this saying, namely, Thou shalt love thy neighbour as thyself.

Love worketh no ill to his neighbour: therefore love is the fulfilling of the law.

ROMANS 13:8-10

For all the law is fulfilled in one word, even in this; Thou shalt love thy neighbor as thyself.

GALATIANS 5:14

If ye fulfill the royal law according to the scripture, Thou shalt love thy neighbour as thyself, ye do well.

JAMES 2:8

DIRECTIVES AND PROMISES

The commandment to love, according to Jesus' interpretation has no limitations: it includes not only neighbours, one another, and the brotherhood, but even enemies.

Ye have heard that it hath been said, Thou shalt love thy neighbour, and hate thine enemy;

But I say unto you, Love your enemies, bless them that curse you, do good to them that hate you, and pray for them which despitefully use you, and persecute you.

MATTHEW 5:43-44

Be ye all of one mind, having compassion one of another, love as brethren, be pitiful, be courteous:

Not rendering evil for evil, or railing for railing: but contrariwise blessing; knowing that ye are thereunto called, that ye should inherit a blessing.

I PETER 3:8-9

We are of God . . . Beloved, let us love one another: for love is of God; and every one that loveth is born of God, and knoweth God.

He that loveth not knoweth not God; for God is love.

I JOHN 4:6-8

[Jesus said:] A new commandment I give unto you, That ye love one another; as I have loved you, that ye also love one another.

By this shall all men know that ye are my disciples, if ye have love one to another.

JOHN 13:34-35

Jesus answered . . . If a man love me, he will keep my words: and my Father will love him, and we will come unto him, and make our abode with him.

JOHN 14:23

Let love be without dissimulation. . . . Be kindly affectioned one to another with brotherly love.

ROMANS 12:9-10

Let this mind be in you, which was also in Christ Jesus.

PHILIPPIANS 2:5

If we love one another, God dwelleth in us, and his love is perfected in us.

I JOHN 4:12

SERVE GOD
(EXODUS 3:12)

What does it mean "to serve God"? *Webster's Collegiate Dictionary* gives some twenty-seven meanings for the verb *to serve*. Only a few are relevant to our thinking here.

I. WORSHIP. One definition given is: "to exert oneself continuously or statedly for: specif., in a religious sense, to obey and worship."

It is interesting to note that in the Bible one of the earliest instances of the phrase "serve God" seems to use the words in the sense of "worship." This is in the story of the burning bush, when Moses was protesting against God's call:

And he [God] said, Certainly I will be with thee; and this shall be a token unto thee, that I have sent thee: When thou hast brought forth the people out of Egypt, ye shall serve God upon this mountain.

EXODUS 3:12

Worship is a part of our service to God, a part that is frequently unrecognized and neglected. Only through worship, opening our hearts continuously to God's presence and direction, can we, his creatures, be enabled to serve him acceptably.

II. OBEDIENCE. Frequently in the Old Testament obedience is recognized as a part of serving God (as it is in the dictionary definition above):

You shall walk after the Lord your God, and fear him, and keep his commandments, and obey his voice, and ye shall serve him, and cleave unto him.

DEUTERONOMY 13:4

In Jesus' time, obedience to the law seems to have been emphasized over and above all other aspects of serving. (Nor have we even today completely freed ourselves from this legalistic interpretation.)

The ritualistic laws had to do with every detail of the daily life: with the washing of the hands, with the repetition of certain prayers, with the touching of the mezzuzah on the doorpost on entering or leaving the house; with what foods to eat, and how to prepare them; with the observance of the sabbath, of feasts and fasts and holy days; with tithing and the giving of offerings and sacrifices; with attendance at synagogue and temple services; and with innumerable other details.

Fearing and loving God were mentioned as parts of this serving, but the overwhelming emphasis seems to have been on the doing of specific acts.

Take diligent heed to do the commandment and the law, which Moses the servant of the Lord charged you, to love the Lord your God, and to walk in all his ways, and to keep his commandments and to cleave unto him, and to serve him with all your heart and with all your soul.

JOSHUA 22:5

III. HUMILITY. One of the dictionary definitions of *to serve* is: "to labor as a servant." This is perhaps the most familiar of the meanings.

We are reminded of Jesus' words to his disciples in which he implies that service to people is service to God:

He that is greatest among you, let him be as the younger; and he that is chief, as he that doth serve. . . .

I am among you as he that serveth.

LUKE 22:26-27

Ye know that they which are accounted to rule over the Gentiles exercise lordship over them; and their great ones exercise authority upon them.

But so shall it not be among you: but whosoever will be great among you, shall be your minister;

And whosoever of you will be the chiefest, shall be the servant of all.

For even the Son of man came not to be ministered unto, but to minister.

MARK 10:42-45

Paul, in his last visit to Ephesus, reminded the elders of the church there of the need for humility in serving the Lord.

Ye know, from the first day that I came into Asia, after what manner I have been with you at all seasons,

Serving the Lord with all humility of mind.

ACTS 20:18-19

Later, in his letter to them written from Rome where he was in prison, these words occur:

I therefore, the prisoner of the Lord, beseech you that ye walk worthy of the vocation wherewith ye are called,

With all lowliness and meekness, with longsuffering, forbearing one another in love;

Endeavouring to keep the unity of the Spirit in the bond of peace.

EPHESIANS 4:1-3

Perhaps the most beautiful description of Christian humility is Paul's tribute to his beloved Master:

Let this mind be in you, which was also in Christ Jesus:

Who, being in the form of God . . . made himself of no reputation, and took upon him the form of a servant, and was made in the likeness of men:

And being found in fashion as a man, he humbled himself, and became obedient unto death, even the death of the cross.

PHILIPPIANS 2:5-8

The need for humility in God's service also finds expression in the Old Testament:

What doth the Lord require of thee, but to do justly, and to love mercy, and to walk humbly with thy God?

MICAH 6:8

IV. PURE MOTIVES. Jesus emphasized that our service to God should be rendered from pure motives.

Take heed that ye do not your alms before men, to be seen of them: otherwise ye have no reward of your Father which is in heaven.

Therefore when thou doest thine alms, do not sound a trumpet before thee, as the hypocrites do in the synagogues and in the streets, that they may have glory of men. Verily I say unto you, they have their reward.

But when thou doest alms, let not thy left hand know what thy right hand doeth.

MATTHEW 6:1-3

V. JOY. Among all the legalistic directives in the Old Testament, it is refreshing to come across a foreshadowing of the New Testament's emphasis on joy as an element of our service to God. The psalmist sings:

Make a joyful noise unto the Lord, all ye lands.

Serve the Lord with gladness: come before his presence with singing.

PSALMS 100:1-2

The early disciples learned through their own experience how joyful the service of the Lord can be:

After these things the Lord appointed other seventy also, and sent them two by two before his face into every city and place, whither he himself would come . . .

And the seventy returned again with joy, saying, Lord, even the devils are subject unto us through thy name.

And he said unto them, I beheld Satan as lightning fall from heaven.

Behold, I give unto you power . . . and nothing shall by any means hurt you.

Notwithstanding in this rejoice not, that the spirits are subject unto you; but rather rejoice, because your names are written in heaven.

LUKE 10: 1,17-20

VI. GENTLENESS. Paul's words to Timothy are still good advice for those of us today who are trying to learn to be servants of God:

Follow righteousness, faith, charity, peace, with them that call on the Lord out of a pure heart.

But foolish and unlearned questions avoid, knowing that they do gender strifes.

And the servant of the Lord must not strive; but be gentle unto all men, apt to teach, patient.

In meekness instructing those that oppose themselves; if God peradventure will give them repentance to the acknowledging of the truth.

II TIMOTHY 2:22-25

VII. COMPASSION. As Jesus drew together the commandments "Love God" and "Love thy neighbor," and gave them almost equal importance, so throughout all his teaching, "service to God" and "service to people" are inseparably united.

Nothing in the Old Testament compares in beauty and depth of spiritual insight with Jesus' parable of the last judgment.* Here was no judgment based on legalistic obedience to rules and regulations; here was a clear and easily understood standard based on compassion for those in need.

Then shall the King say unto them on his right hand, Come, ye blessed of my Father, inherit the kingdom prepared for you from the foundation of the world:

For I was an hungered, and ye gave me meat: I was thirsty, and ye gave me drink: I was a stranger, and ye took me in:

Naked, and ye clothed me: I was sick, and ye visited me: I was in prison, and ye came unto me.

Then shall the righteous answer him, saying, Lord, when saw we thee an hungered, and fed thee? or thirsty, and gave thee drink?

When saw we thee a stranger, and took thee in? or naked, and clothed thee?

Or when saw we thee sick, or in prison, and came unto thee?

And the King shall answer and say unto them, Verily I say unto you, Inasmuch as ye have done it unto one of the least of these my brethren, ye have done it unto me.

MATTHEW 25:34-40

---

* Matthew 25:31-46.

Worship, obedience, humility, pure motives, joy, gentleness, compassion—true service to God includes all these.

Those of us who are parents, responsible for the spiritual welfare of a family, would do well to read and take to heart the story in the last chapter of Joshua. The Israelites have at last come home to the long-promised land. Joshua is reminding them of all that God has done for them. And he concludes:

Now therefore fear the Lord, and serve him in sincerity and in truth. . . .

And if it seem evil unto you to serve the Lord, choose you this day whom ye will serve . . .; but as for me and my house, we will serve the Lord.

JOSHUA 24:14-15

DIRECTIVES AND PROMISES

In Deuteronomy, there is a warning against the dangers of an affluent society that we do well to heed, here in America today:

And it shall be, when the Lord thy God shall have brought thee into the land which he sware unto thy fathers, to Abraham, to Isaac, and to Jacob, to give thee great and goodly cities, which thou buildest not.

And houses full of all good things which thou filledst not, and wells digged, which thou diggedst not, vineyards and olive trees which thou plantedst not: when thou shalt have eaten and be full;

Then beware lest thou forget the Lord, which brought thee forth out of the land of Egypt, from the house of bondage.

Thou shalt fear the Lord thy God, and serve him.

DEUTERONOMY 6:10-13

Samuel said unto the people, Fear not: ye have done all this wickedness: yet turn not aside from following the Lord, but serve the Lord with all your heart;

And turn ye not aside: for then should ye go after vain things, which cannot profit nor deliver, for they are vain. . . .

. . . but I will teach you the good and the right way:

Only fear the Lord, and serve him in truth with all your heart; for consider how great things he hath done for you.

I SAMUEL 12:20-24

Not long before his death, King David gave this advice to his son:

And thou, Solomon my son, know thou the God of thy father, and serve him with a perfect heart and with a willing mind: for the Lord searcheth all hearts, and understandeth all the imaginations of the thoughts: if thou seek him, he will be found of thee; but if thou forsake him, he will cast thee off for ever.

I CHRONICLES 28:9

Now yield your members servants to righteousness unto holiness.

For when ye were the servants of sin, ye were free from righteousness.

What fruit had ye then in those things whereof ye are now ashamed? for the end of those things is death.

But now being made free from sin, and become servants to God, ye have your fruit unto holiness, and the end everlasting life.

ROMANS 6:19-22

And whatsoever ye do, do it heartily, as to the Lord, and not unto men; . . . for ye serve the Lord Christ.

COLOSSIANS 3:23-24

RESPONSES

God, grant that I may serve in newness of spirit, and not in the oldness of the letter. Amen.

SEE: ROMANS 7:6

Enable me, O Lord my God, to present my body a living sacrifice, holy, acceptable unto thee, which is my reasonable service. Amen.

SEE: ROMANS 12:1

Holy Father, grant that we, receiving a kingdom which cannot be moved, may have grace, whereby we may serve thee acceptably with reverence and godly fear. Amen.

SEE: HEBREWS 12:28

REJOICE
(PHILIPPIANS 4:4)

One last word of God to us from the pages of the Bible: "Rejoice!" And this is perhaps the hardest of God's commands for us to obey. But the word is repeated over and over, both in the Old Testament and the New.

We are accustomed to thinking that rejoicing comes to us as a result of outward circumstances. We are slow to recognize it as a by-product of a right relationship to God. Actually, the circumstances of our lives have little to do with the state of our spirits.

Habakkuk had made this discovery when he wrote the following sturdy declaration of his own joyousness:

Although the fig tree shall not blossom, neither shall fruit be in the vines; the labour of the olive shall fail, and the fields shall yield no meat; the flock shall be cut off from the fold, and there shall be no herd in the stalls;

Yet I will rejoice in the Lord, I will joy in the God of my salvation.

HABAKKUK 3:17-18

DIRECTIVES AND PROMISES

How beautiful upon the mountains are the feet of him that bringeth good tidings, that publisheth peace; that bringeth good tidings of good, that publisheth salvation; that saith unto Zion, Thy God reigneth!

Break forth into joy, sing together . . . for the Lord hath comforted his people, he hath redeemed Jerusalem.

ISAIAH 52:7,9

Thou shalt rejoice in every good thing which the Lord thy God hath given unto thee, and unto thine house.

DEUTERONOMY 26:11

Let the heart of them rejoice that seek the Lord.

Seek the Lord and his strength, seek his face continually. . . .

Glory and honour are in his presence; strength and gladness are in his place. . . .

Let the heavens be glad, and let the earth rejoice: and let men say among the nations, The Lord reigneth.

I CHRONICLES 16:10-11,27,31

Let all those that put their trust in thee rejoice: let them ever shout for joy . . . let them also that love thy name be joyful in thee.

PSALMS 5:11

Light is sown for the righteous, and gladness for the upright in heart.

Rejoice in the Lord, ye righteous, and give thanks at the remembrance of his holiness.

PSALMS 97:11-12

Rejoice in the Lord. . . .

For we are the circumcision, which worship God in the spirit, and rejoice in Christ Jesus.

PHILIPPIANS 3:1,3

Rejoice in the Lord alway: and again I say, Rejoice.

PHILIPPIANS 4:4

Rejoice evermore . . .

In every thing give thanks: for this is the will of God in Christ Jesus concerning you.

I THESSALONIANS 5:16,18

RESPONSES

Thou hast put gladness in my heart.

PSALMS 4:7

My heart shall rejoice in thy salvation.

I will sing unto the Lord, because he hath dealt bountifully with me.

PSALMS 13:5-6

The Lord is the portion of mine inheritance and of my cup: thou maintainest my lot.

The lines are fallen unto me in pleasant places; yea, I have a goodly heritage. . . .

I have set the Lord always before me: because he is at my right hand, I shall not be moved.

Therefore my heart is glad, and my glory rejoiceth . . .

Thou wilt show me the path of life: in thy presence is fulness of joy; at thy right hand there are pleasures for evermore.

PSALMS 16:5-6,8-9,11

Thou hast turned for me my mourning into dancing; thou hast put off my sackcloth, and girded me with gladness;

To the end that my glory may sing praise unto thee, and not be silent. O Lord, my God, I will give thanks unto thee forever.

PSALMS 30:11-12

Make us glad according to the days wherein thou hast afflicted us, and the years wherein we have seen evil.

PSALMS 90:15

This is the day which the Lord hath made; we will rejoice and be glad in it.

PSALMS 118:24

The Lord hath done great things for us, whereof we are glad.

PSALMS 126:3

CONCLUSION: GOD'S WORDS THROUGH US

IF WE HAVE BECOME SINCERE FOLLOWERS OF JESUS, "BORN-again Christians," whose hearts are open to God's words to us in the Bible, and also in the circumstances of our lives; if we have truly entered into "the joy of the Lord" and have learned to praise and give thanks in everything; if we have learned to seek him, to obey him, to love him, to serve him, and to rejoice —then we have reached the place in our spiritual life where God can *speak through us* to people whose lives touch ours, where he can anoint us as his prophets, spokesmen for him. Then he can put into our mouths the words he wants us to speak in every changing situation of our lives.

The mere idea of this possibility staggers our imagination and leaves us awed and humble. And yet this is exactly what the scriptures are telling us.

Consider Moses:

Now Moses kept the flock of Jethro his father in law, the priest of Midian: and he led the flock to the backside of the desert, and came to the mountain of God, even to Horeb.

EXODUS 3:1

And there Moses saw the burning bush that burned with fire but was not consumed, and he turned aside to see the strange sight.

Then it was that God spoke to Moses and called him to be his instrument for leading the Israelites out of slavery. But Moses was appalled!

And Moses said unto God, Who am I, that I should go unto Pharaoh, and that I should bring forth the children of Israel out of Egypt?

EXODUS 3:11

And after much further conversation and great reluctance on Moses' part to undertake this mission, he made one final protest:

O my Lord, I am not eloquent, neither heretofore, nor since thou hast spoken unto thy servant: but I am slow of speech, and of a slow tongue.

And the Lord said unto him, Who hath made man's mouth? or who maketh the dumb, or deaf, or the seeing, or the blind? have not I the Lord?

Now therefore go, and I will be with thy mouth, and teach thee what thou shalt say.

EXODUS 4:10-12

Remember also Isaiah.

He recognized as a gift from God whatever wisdom he had. He wrote:

The Lord God hath given me the tongue of the learned, that I should know how to speak a word in season to him that is weary: he wakeneth morning by morning, he wakeneth mine ear to hear as the learned.

The Lord God hath opened mine ear, and I was not rebellious, neither turned away back.

ISAIAH 50:4-5

Consider also Jeremiah.

Then the word of the Lord came unto me, saying,

Before thou camest forth out of the womb, I sanctified thee, and I ordained thee a prophet unto the nations.

JEREMIAH 1:4-5

Jeremiah, like Moses, protested:

Then said I, Ah, Lord God! behold, I cannot speak: for I am a child.

But the Lord said unto me, Say not, I am a child: for thou shalt go to all that I shall send thee, and whatsoever I command thee thou shalt speak.

Be not afraid of their faces: for I am with thee to deliver thee, saith the Lord.

Then the Lord put forth his hand, and touched my mouth. And the Lord said unto me, Behold, I have put my words in thy mouth.

JEREMIAH 1:6-9

Consider next Ezekiel. He too, like Isaiah, had a strange and shining vision.

And when I saw it, I fell upon my face, and I heard a voice of one that spake.

And he said unto me, Son of man, I send thee to the children of Israel, to a rebellious nation that hath rebelled against me. . . .

And thou, son of man, be not afraid of them, neither be afraid of their words, though briers and thorns be with thee, and thou dost dwell among scorpions: be not afraid of their words, nor be dismayed at their looks, though they be a rebellious house.

And thou shalt speak my words unto them, whether they will hear or whether they will forbear. . . .

But thou, son of man, hear what I say unto thee; Be not thou rebellious like that rebellious house: open thy mouth, and eat that I give thee.

And when I looked, behold, an hand was sent unto me; and, lo, a roll of a book was therein . . .

Moreover he said unto me, Son of man, eat that thou findest; eat this roll, and go speak . . .

Then did I eat it; and it was in my mouth as honey for sweetness.

EZEKIEL 1:28; 2:1,3,6-9; 3:1-3

The New Testament repeats the promise that God will put his words in the mouths of those who yield themselves to him. When Jesus was talking to his twelve disciples, before he sent them forth to be witnesses for him,

. . he gave them power against unclean spirits, to cast them out, and to heal all manner of sickness and all manner of disease . . .

[And he said:] Behold, I send you forth as sheep in the midst of wolves: be ye therefore wise as serpents, and harmless as doves.

But beware of men: for they will deliver you up to the councils, and they will scourge you in their synagogues;

And ye shall be brought before governors and kings for my sake, for a testimony against them and the Gentiles.

But when they deliver you up, take no thought how or what ye shall speak, for it shall be given you in that same hour what ye shall speak.

For it is not ye that speak, but the Spirit of your Father which speaketh in you.

MATTHEW 10:1,16-20

It is true that few of us are called to be spokesmen for God to the nations of the world. It is equally true as we study God's Word to us, that God's concern for the nations does not contradict nor interefere with *his concern for individuals.* This is perhaps the deepest spiritual insight in Jesus' gospel.

Since this is so, it is obvious that God needs not only prophets to speak his words to the nations, but also innumerable spokesmen to speak his words to individuals, in all the crowded corners of the earth. He needs a spokesman *wherever you are, in the precise situation in which you find yourself, now.*

Prophets of death are everywhere! They speak words of doubt and unbelief; of fear and anxiety; of desperation and despair; of suspicion and cynicism.

Every dedicated follower of Jesus, on the other hand, may learn, as his disciple, to be a prophet ministering life to all around him—speaking God's words of faith, hope, courage, love and joy.

James said:

But the tongue can no man tame.

JAMES 3:8

And he spoke truly. No man *can* tame the tongue. Only God, the Creator, can do so. He speaks to each one of us as he did to Moses:

Who hath made man's mouth? . . . have not I, the Lord?

Now therefore go, and I will be with thy mouth, and teach thee what thou shalt say.

EXODUS 4:11-12

Surely our response to God's call for spokesmen and to his promises of guidance, must be an ever-growing attentiveness to hear his words to us, in order that we may in turn speak his words "with boldness."

[Peter prayed:] And now, Lord, behold their threatenings: and grant unto thy servants, that with all boldness they may speak thy word. . . .

And when they had prayed, the place was shaken where they were assembled together; and they were all filled with the Holy Ghost, and they spake the word of God with boldness.

ACTS 4:29,31

It is helpful to call to mind the faithful testimony of other humble spokesmen for God through the ages.

There was Balaam who declared:

If Balak would give me his house full of silver and gold, I cannot go beyond the commandment of the Lord, to do either good or bad of my own mind; but what the Lord saith, that will I speak.

NUMBERS 24:13

Then there was Micaiah who, standing boldly before the kings of Judah and of Israel, said:

As the Lord liveth, what the Lord saith unto me, that will I speak.

I KINGS 22:14

And we remember again Peter and John, when they had been arrested and brought before the council.

And they commanded them not to speak at all nor teach in the name of Jesus.

But Peter and John answered and said unto them, Whether it be right in the sight of God to hearken unto you more than unto God, judge ye.

For we cannot but speak the things which we have seen and heard.

ACTS 4:18-20

We need to pray daily, and sometimes hourly:

Holy Father: open thou mine ears and my heart, that I may clearly discern thy words to me.

Put, I pray thee, thy words in my mouth, and enable me to speak them boldly.

Bridle my tongue by thine own power, and grant that by the grace of thy Spirit within me, I may speak "the truth in love."*

Enable me, more and more, to grow in the ability to minister life—to speak thy words of faith, and hope, and joy, and the assurance of thine everlasting love for each one of us, thy creatures: in the name of thy Son, Jesus, thy Word made flesh, our Lord and Saviour. Amen.

---

* Ephesians 4:15.

INDEX OF
BIBLE QUOTATIONS